Patrick Keiller
The Possibility of Life's Survival on the Planet

Tate Publishing

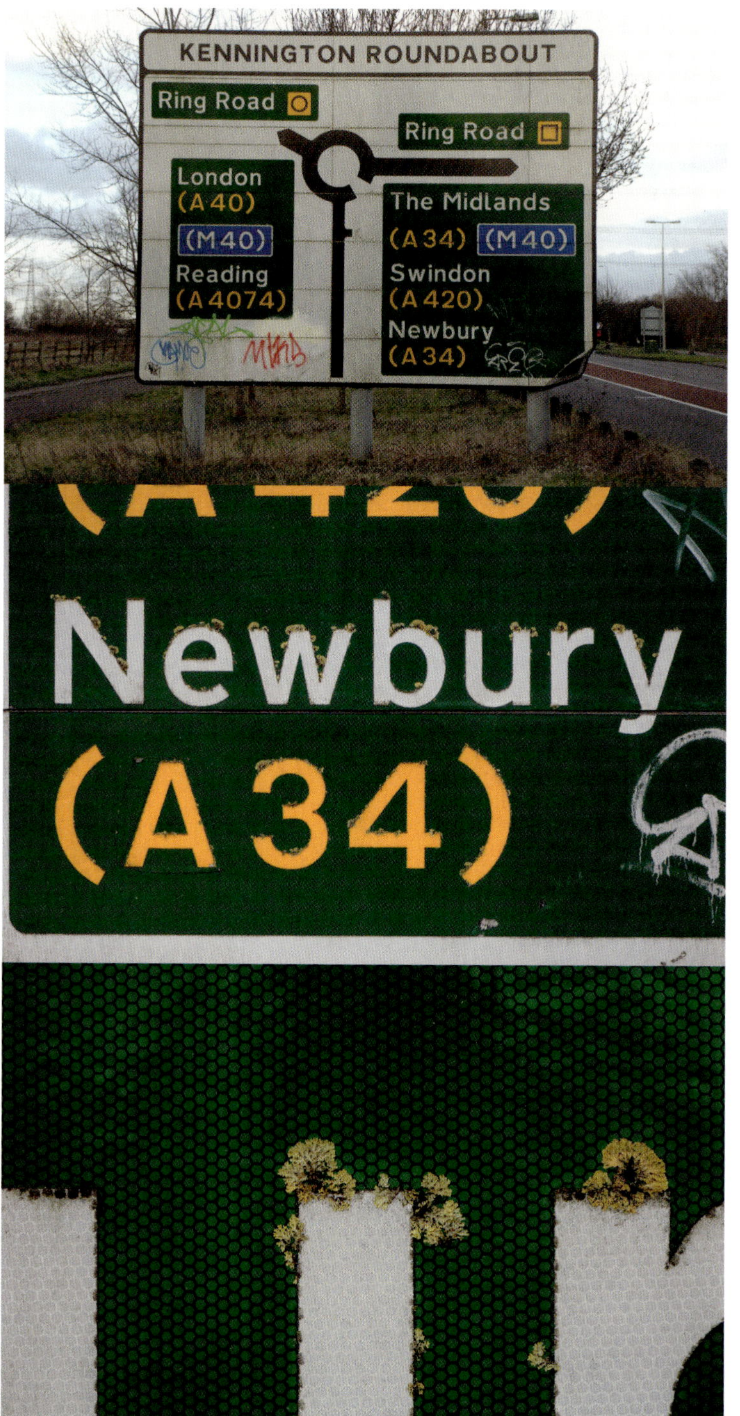
KENNINGTON ROUNDABOUT
Ring Road
Ring Road
London
(A 40)
(M40)
Reading
(A 4074)
The Midlands
(A 34) (M40)
Swindon
(A 420)
Newbury
(A 34)
Newbury
(A 34)

Robinsonism

In August 2010, I completed a film[1] that begins with a series of captions:
'A few years ago, while dismantling a derelict caravan in the corner of a field, a
recycling worker found a box containing 19 film cans and a notebook. / Researchers
have arranged some of this material as a film, narrated by their institution's
co-founder, with the title / *Robinson in Ruins*. / The wandering it describes began
on 22 January 2008.' According to the film's narrator, its footage had been
photographed by a wandering, erratic scholar on a journey through landscapes
in the south of England, and the researchers' institution had been set up
some years earlier 'with the aim of developing novel definitions of economic
wellbeing, based on the transformative potential we attributed to images of
landscape'. While making the film, I had hoped that, in future, I might also
arrange the material in other ways, and an opportunity to do so was offered
by an invitation to devise an exhibit at Tate Britain that would include works
from the Tate's collection. The resulting installation was *The Robinson Institute*,
which revisited the journey described by the film, combining a selection of
its images with historical and other works suggested by their subjects and their
fictional cinematographer's concerns. In this book, a similar sequence of images
is accompanied by a written commentary.

....

1. *Robinson in Ruins* (101mins, 35mm to DCP, 2010)

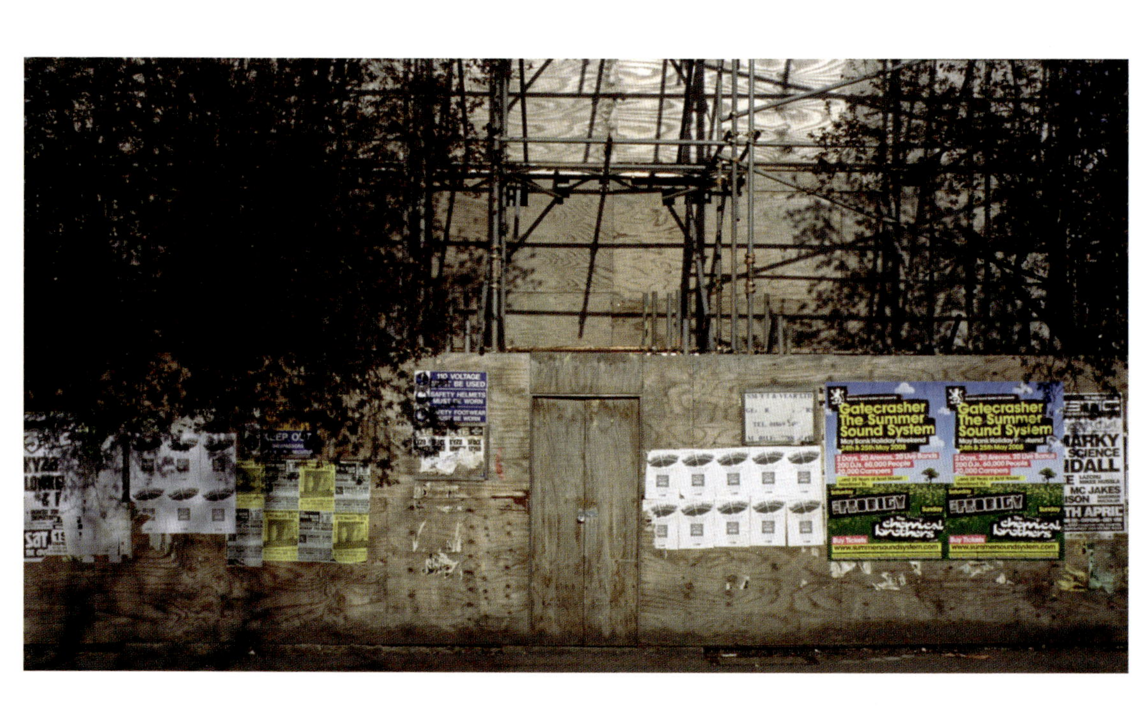
110 VOLTAGE
MUST BE USED
SAFETY HELMETS
MUST BE WORN
SAFETY FOOTWEAR
MUST BE WORN
KEEP OUT
Gatecrasher
The Summer
Sound System
May Bank Holiday Weekend
24th & 25th May 2008
2 Days, 20 Arenas, 20 Live Bands
200 DJs, 60,000 People
10,000 Campers
PRODIGY
Sunday
chemical brothers
Buy Tickets
www.summersoundsystem.com
Gatecrasher
The Summer
Sound System
May Bank Holiday Weekend
24th & 25th May 2008
2 Days, 20 Arenas, 20 Live Bands
200 DJs, 60,000 People
10,000 Campers
PRODIGY
Sunday
chemical brothers
Buy Tickets
www.summersoundsystem.com
MARKY
SCIENCE
IDALL
MC JAKES
ISON
TH APRIL
SAT

Robinson

In the film, the introductory captions are followed by an image of a structure of plywood and scaffolding erected around an empty nineteenth-century neo-Gothic house, accompanied by a first line of narration: 'When a man called Robinson was released from Edgcott open prison, he made his way to the nearest city, and looked for somewhere to haunt.'

Nothing had been heard of this fictional individual since his disappearance in November 1995, following events described towards the end of a previous film of which he is the unseen protagonist, *Robinson in Space* (1997),[2] until an opportunity arose to release him from fictional incarceration. During ten months of 2008, I had photographed about four hours of 35 mm negative of landscape and similar subjects encountered mostly in a slow, elliptical progress through part of southern England, intending to arrange the edited footage as the document of a journey by someone who had set out in the belief that, by making it, he or she would bring about some kind of transformation. To begin with, the film had not necessarily involved anyone called Robinson, but when I began to write its script, in March 2009, I decided that it would, and that I would call it *Robinson in Ruins*.

Robinson in Ruins: house,
plywood and scaffolding

2. *Robinson in Space* (82 mins, 35 mm, 1997)

Robinson in Space was itself the sequel to the earlier *London* (1994),[3] in which
the fictional, unseen Robinson was first encountered, then a part-time lecturer
at the University of Barking engaged in a study of 'the problem of London': at
the beginning of 1992, he asked his former lover, the film's unnamed, similarly
unseen narrator, whose words were spoken by Paul Scofield, to accompany
him on a series of journeys about the city. It had seemed to me that Robinson
was a name that someone who wasn't English might choose, either for a
fictional character, or for themselves, should they wish to adopt an English
name. It is found in many non-English contexts: the French words *robinson*
(a large umbrella; a person who lives alone, apart from the world), *robinsoniser*,
robinsonisme, robinsonade, and the verb *robinsonner,* the latter coined by
Arthur Rimbaud; Samuel Robinson was the pseudonym adopted in exile by
the Venezuelan philosopher and educator Simón Rodríguez (1769–1854),
Simón Bolivar's tutor, after whom one of Venezuela's present-day anti-poverty
initiatives, the *Misión Robinson*, is named. I took the name from Kafka's
Amerika, in which the protagonist Karl Rossmann encounters two itinerants,
Delamarche and Robinson, who describe themselves as out-of-work mechanics
and subsequently cause difficulties for Karl, by then employed as a hotel lift boy.
Kafka's Robinson is Irish, which prompts the hotel's head waiter to exclaim:
'I don't even believe that his name is Robinson, for no Irishman was ever called
that since Ireland was Ireland'.[4]

In January 1998, having also narrated *Robinson in Space*, Paul Scofield sent
me a postcard of August Sander's 1929 photograph *Itinerants*, which he had
seen in an exhibition. In Paul's absence, I had the idea that the figure on the
left slightly resembled him, and perhaps, even more slightly, Harun Farocki,
who plays the character Delamarche in *Klassenverhältnisse*, Jean-Marie Straub
and Danièlle Huillet's adaptation of the novel, while the figure on the right
looked a little like Manfred Blank, who plays Straub and Huillet's Robinson,
and so might also resemble my unseen protagonist. More recently, I have
imagined he might look quite different.

3. *London* (85mins, 35mm, 1994)
4. Franz Kafka, *America*, introduced by Edwin Muir,
London 2005, p.165.

August Sander
***Vagrants* 1929**

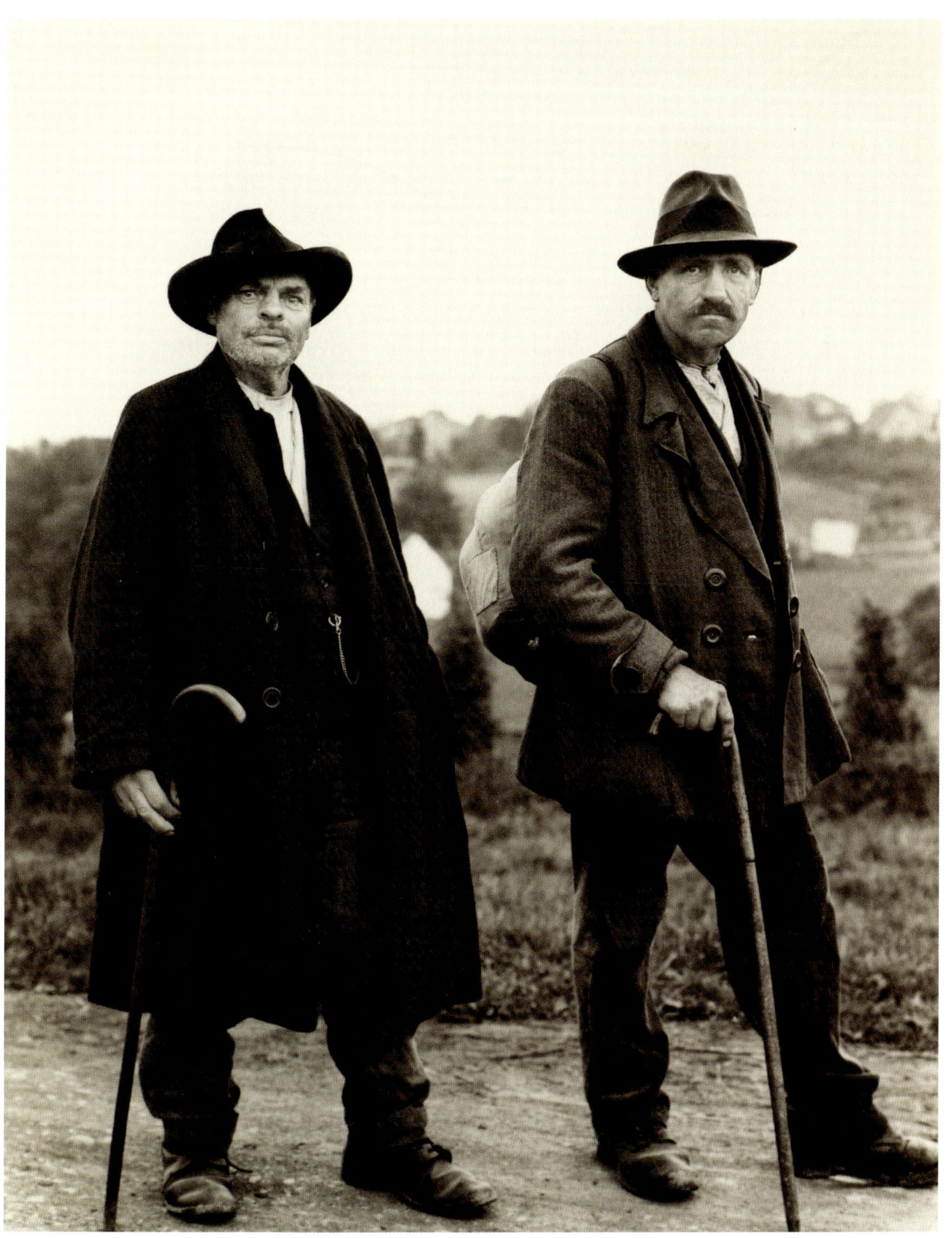

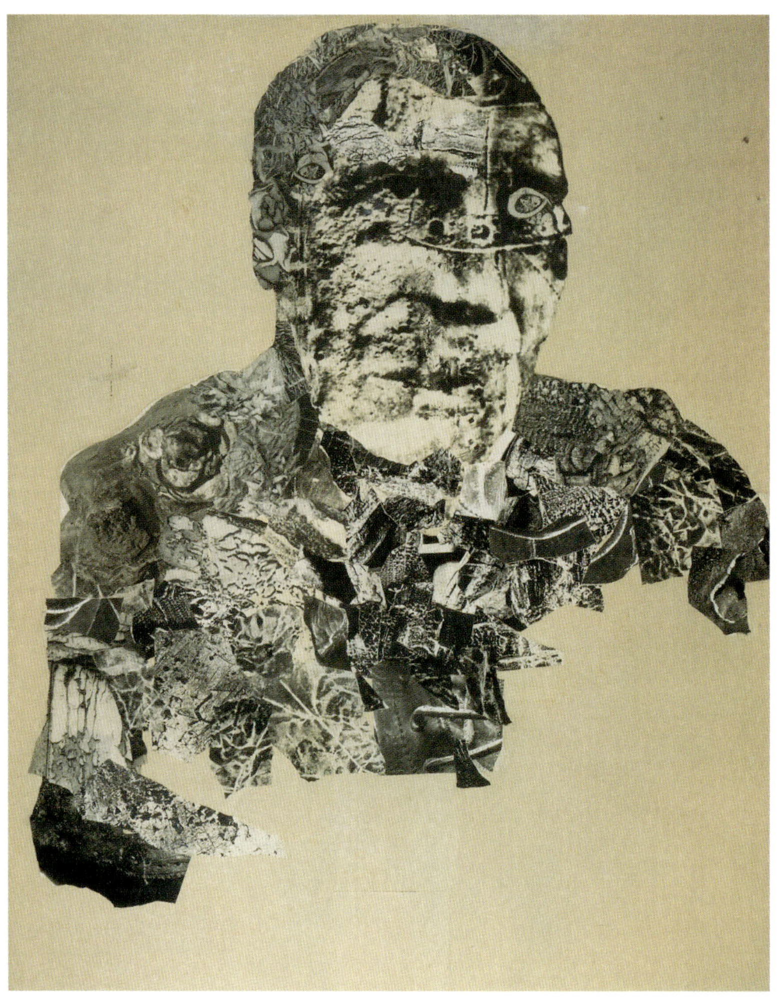

Robinson was devised to enable a first-person narrator to explore ideas one might entertain but would not necessarily adopt, at least not wholeheartedly, and is hence, sometimes, a parody: *London*, for example, could be described as a joke about a man who thinks he would be happier if London were more like Paris, or more like his imagination of Paris. His critique was informed by works both by and about European writers who had visited London, including Alexander Herzen, Guillaume Apollinaire, Rimbaud and Paul Verlaine. The latter two read Edgar Allan Poe's *Narrative of Arthur Gordon Pym of Nantucket*, which they knew from Baudelaire's translation, to improve their English, and visited the Reading Room of the British Museum.

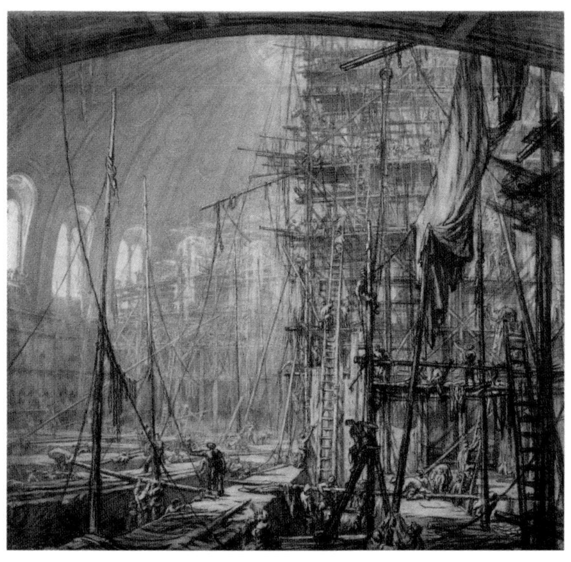

Handing over the responsibility for ideas to someone other than the narrator seemed to make it easier for the films to examine or, occasionally, promote them: in each film Robinson attempted to better understand a perceived 'problem' by looking at, and making images of, landscape. In *London*, the city's physical and social shortcomings were attributed, in the end, to its lack of metropolitan government and lengthy occupation by the representatives of global capital. In *Robinson in Space*, the spatial and other impoverishments accompanying the decline of production were discovered to be symptomatic not of economic failure, but of the successful operation of an unattractive economic model. *Robinson in Ruins* was part of a non-fictional academic research project,[5] prompted by 'a perceived discrepancy between, on one hand, the critical and cultural attention devoted to experience of mobility and displacement and, on the other, a tendency to fall back on formulations of *dwelling* derived from a more settled, agricultural past.'

Nigel Henderson
Head of a Man 1956

Muirhead Bone
The British Museum Reading Room May 1907 1907

5. The Future of Landscape and the Moving Image, a three-year project in the Arts and Humanities Research Council's Landscape and Environment Programme, a collaboration between Patrick Keiller, formerly Research Fellow at the Royal College of Art, Patrick Wright, Professor of Literature and Visual & Material Culture, Kings College London, Doreen Massey, Emeritus Professor of Geography at the Open University, and doctoral researcher Matthew Flintham, whose companion project was 'Parallel Landscapes: A Spatial and Critical Study of Militarised Sites in the United Kingdom'.

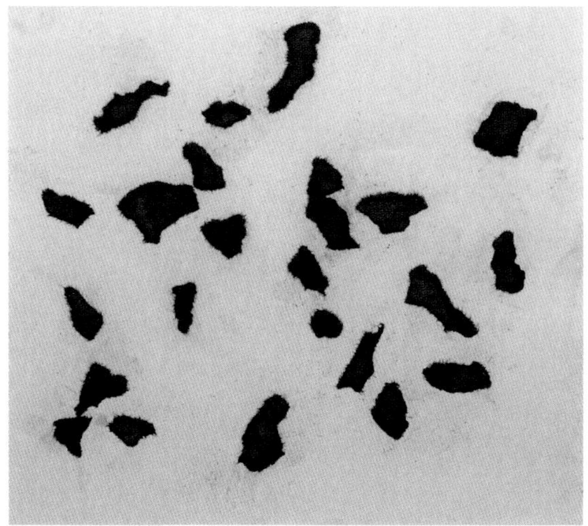

The journey evolved in an exploratory manner, so that a camera subject was often determined by a chance encounter, sometimes only after having visited its predecessor. After ten months, the camera had mapped out an approximately elliptical, anti-clockwise progress.

The ruins were of four kinds: architectural, in that a surprising number of the locations encountered were, in one way or another, ruins; personal, in that, by then, Robinson seemed physically depleted, if not actually a ghost; ecological, in that, in the narrative, he is enlisted by non-human intelligences anxious to preserve a long-term future for the biosphere; and economic, in that the film had been photographed during 2008, the year of long-awaited neoliberal crisis, its cinematography continuing until mid-November. During the autumn of that year, it had seemed possible that the crisis might lead to lasting change. For Robert Wade, for example, in an essay 'Financial Regime Change?', dated 7 October 2008,[6]

6. Robert Wade, 'Financial Regime Change?', *New Left Review*, no.53, September–October 2008, pp.5–21.

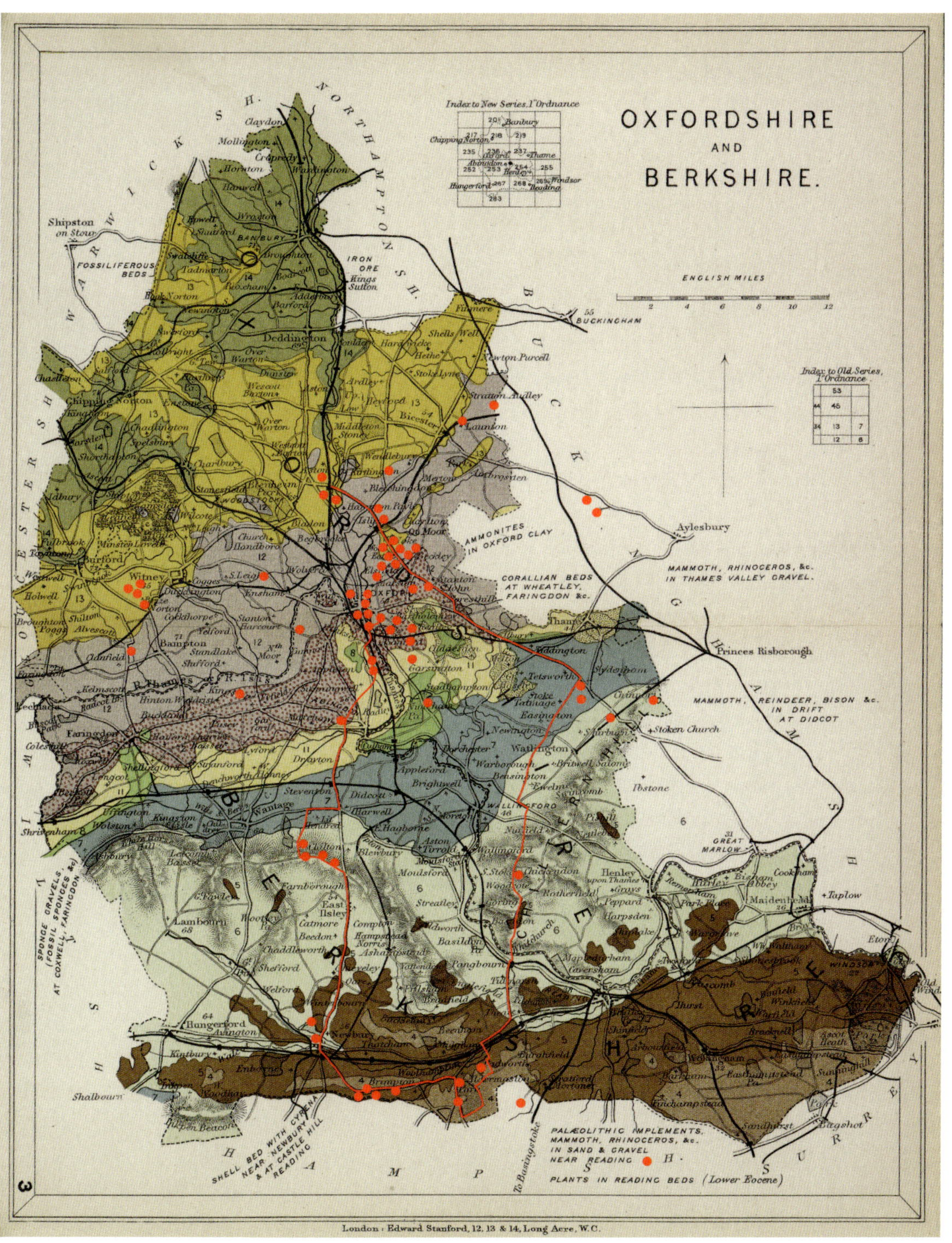

OXFORDSHIRE
AND
BERKSHIRE.

Index to New Series 1" Ordnance
Index to Old Series, 1" Ordnance.

ENGLISH MILES

London: Edward Stanford, 12, 13 & 14, Long Acre, W.C.

FOSSILIFEROUS BEDS
IRON ORE
AMMONITES IN OXFORD CLAY
CORALLIAN BEDS AT WHEATLEY, FARINGDON &c.
MAMMOTH, RHINOCEROS, &c. IN THAMES VALLEY GRAVEL.
MAMMOTH, REINDEER, BISON &c. IN DRIFT AT DIDCOT
SPONGE GRAVELS (FOSSIL SPONGES &c.) AT COXWELL, FARINGDON
SHELL BED WITH CYPRINA NEAR NEWBURY & AT CASTLE HILL READING
PALÆOLITHIC IMPLEMENTS, MAMMOTH, RHINOCEROS, &c. IN SAND & GRAVEL NEAR READING
PLANTS IN READING BEDS (Lower Eocene)

Buckingham
Aylesbury
Princes Risborough
Banbury
Oxford
Witney
Wantage
Hungerford
Newbury
Reading
Maidenhead
Eton
Windsor
Henley upon Thames
Great Marlow

Governmental responses to the crisis further suggest that we have entered the second leg of Polanyi's 'double movement', the recurrent pattern in capitalism whereby (to oversimplify) a regime of free markets and increasing commodification generates such suffering and displacement as to prompt attempts to impose closer regulation of markets and de-commodification ... The first leg of the current double movement was the long reign of neoliberalism and its globalization consensus. The second as yet has no name, and may turn out to be a period marked more by a lack of agreement than any new consensus.

In May 2009, pressed for a preliminary description of the film, I offered: 'In early 2008, a marginalised individual sets out to avert global catastrophe, hoping to trigger the end of neoliberalism by going for a walk', which got a laugh, but in the end I didn't use the line, partly because it seemed to give away too much about the narrative, but also because, by then, it did not seem particularly funny. As Wade had continued:

> Some caution is in order. There is a recurrent cycle of debate in the wake of financial crises, as an initial outpouring of radical proposals gives way to incremental muddling through, followed by resumption of normal business.

It had seemed to me that England's, or the UK's, landscape would be an appropriate context in which to examine the tensions between dwelling and displacement. I understood the latter, primarily, as characteristic of capitalist development, beginning with the agrarian capitalism that originated in the south of England at about the same time that England began to embark on colonial expansion. Of the more recent period, Wade wrote:

> The UK's role in the crisis deserves emphasis, because contrary to conventional wisdom, the dynamics at its heart started there. The Thatcher government set out to attract financial business from New York by advertising London as a place where US firms could escape onerous domestic regulation. The government of Tony Blair and Chancellor Gordon Brown continued the strategy, leading Brown to boast that the UK had 'not only light but limited regulation'.

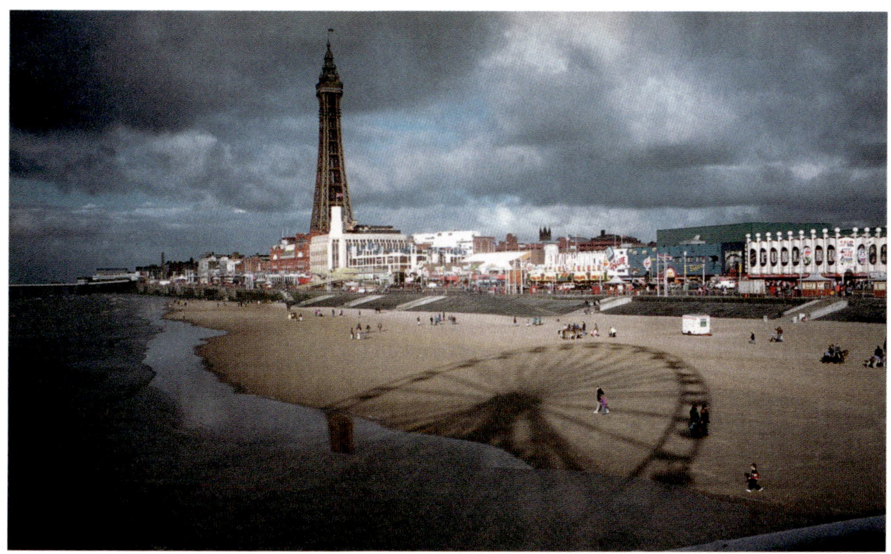

Robinson, too, seemed emblematically displaced, especially since his incarceration. Towards the end of the previous film, the narrator had let slip that Blackpool was Robinson's 'home town', and that 'his parents used to have a nursery which specialised in strains of giant vegetables',[7] an attempt to evoke Don Siegel's *Invasion of the Body Snatchers* (1956) and a reference to an actual nursery, nearby. In *Robinson in Ruins*, the narrator quotes Shelley: 'All things have a home but one – Thou, Oh, Englishman, hast none!' from *The Masque of Anarchy*, written on hearing of the massacre at Peterloo in Manchester in August 1819, and continues: 'Of course, Robinson wasn't his real name, and he wasn't English. He had arrived in London in 1966, from Berlin, before which his history was uncertain, having been attracted by the period's popular culture, and the presence of so many prehistoric structures in the landscape.'

Julie Norris
Blackpool from Central Pier 1994

7. Patrick Keiller, *Robinson in Space*, London 1999, p.187.

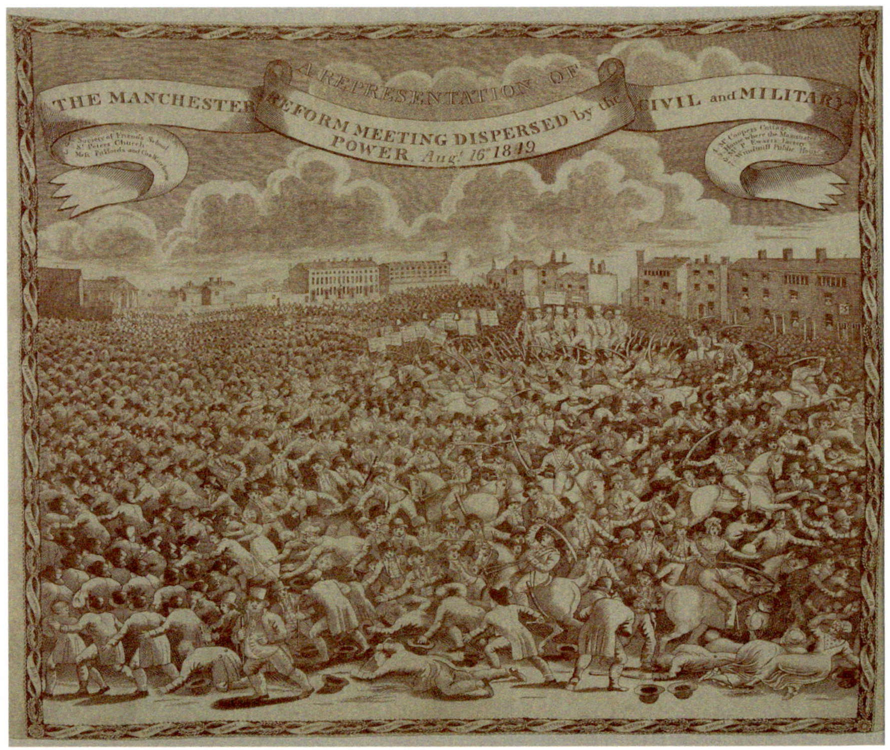

Near the beginning of the film, the narration includes: 'In the library, he
photocopied [Fredric] Jameson's anticipation of the crisis: "It seems to be easier
for us today to imagine the thoroughgoing deterioration of the earth, and of
nature, than the breakdown of late capitalism; perhaps that is due to some failure
of our imagination."[8] ... From a nearby car park, he surveyed the centre of the
island on which he was shipwrecked: "the location", he wrote, "of a *Great Malady*,
that I shall dispel, in the manner of Turner, by making *picturesque views*, on
journeys to sites of scientific and historic interest".' The car park is in Oxford,
'a centre masquerading as a margin',[9] so that the *Great Malady* – first encountered
in *London* as Baudelaire's 'horror of one's home'[10] – might be attributed in this
case to the predominantly Anglo-American failure of imagination alluded to by
Jameson, and hence to neoliberalism itself.

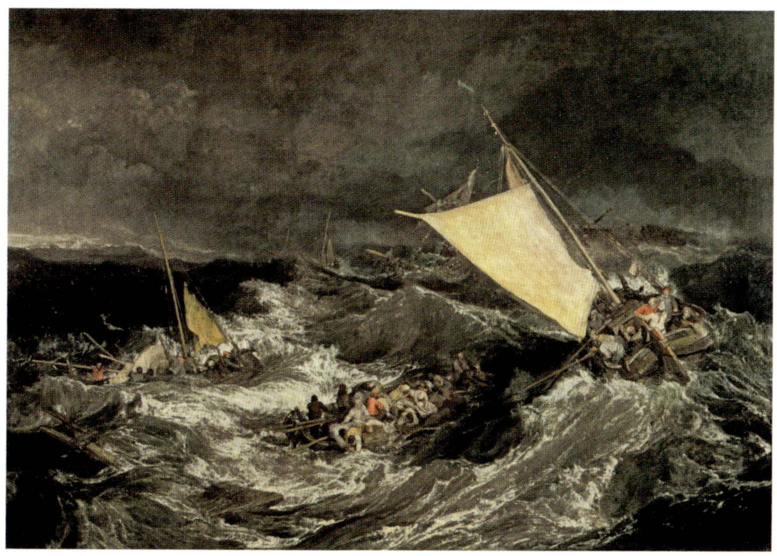

In *The Production of Space*, Henri Lefebvre identifies a 'conceptual triad' of *spatial practice, representations of space* and *representational space. Spatial practice,* he writes, 'embodies a close association, within perceived space, between daily reality (daily routine) and urban reality (the routes and networks which link up the places set aside for work, "private life" and leisure)'. *Representations of space* include 'the space of scientists, planners, urbanists, technocratic subdividers and social engineers, as of a certain type of artist with a scientific bent – all of whom identify what is lived and what is perceived with what is conceived … This is the dominant space in any society (or mode of production).' *Representational space* is 'space as directly *lived* through its associated images and symbols, and hence the space of 'inhabitants' and 'users', but also of some artists and perhaps of those, such as a few writers and philosophers, who *describe* and aspire to do no more than describe. This is the dominated – and hence passively experienced – space which the imagination seeks to change and appropriate.'[11]

---

after John Slack
Handkerchief commemorating
the Peterloo massacre, 16 August
1819

J.M.W. Turner
The Shipwreck **exhibited 1805**

8. Fredric Jameson, *The Seeds of Time*, New York 1996, p.xi.
9. Terry Eagleton, review of Isaiah Berlin, *Enlightening: Letters 1946–1960*, in *Guardian*, 27 June 2009.
10. Charles Baudelaire, *Intimate Journals*, translated by Christopher Isherwood, London 1949, p.37: 'My Heart Laid Bare', LVIII.
11. Henri Lefebvre: *The Production of Space*, translated by Donald Nicholson-Smith, Oxford 1991, pp.38–9.

I interpreted these three descriptions to mean that, while everyday
activities such as looking out of the window, or walking in the street, might
be construed as *spatial practice*, and the designers of a building, or a new
city, might be engaged in producing *representations of space*, if one seeks, in
some imaginative way, such as writing, making images, or making films,
to change and appropriate space, one is dealing with *representational space*.
Moreover, if *representational space* admits the possibility of change through
effort by, and works of, the imagination, then it might be possible, not only
to dispel a *Malady* 'in the manner of Turner' by making *picturesque views*, as
in making the film, but to do so also by exhibiting artworks and other items,
and reproducing images of them, such as those included here, all this 'with
the aim of developing novel definitions of economic wellbeing, based on the
transformative potential we attributed to images of landscape'.

In *Robinson in Space*, Robinson had been commissioned to research the
problem of England, not specified, but seemingly something to do with the
claimed decline of manufacturing industry. He and his companion narrator
set out to explore the UK's material economy, discovering a surprisingly
successful manufacturing sector, much of it owned by non-UK companies,
and visiting most of England's larger ports, until they began to discern an older,
deeper structure beneath the then-buoyant consumer economy: the military
aspect of the nation state and, with it, the US-UK relationship. During the
last few weeks of the journey, they encountered a variety of military-industrial
sites, including several British Aerospace (now BAE Systems) aircraft factories:
at Brough, near Hull; Samlesbury, near Preston; the cleared site of another
factory in Preston, then recently demolished, and Warton, a few miles west,
where the Tornado aircraft was produced; in Barrow-in-Furness, the former
Vickers shipyard – then owned by GEC, whose weapons production later
merged with BAE – was building the Trident submarines, the third of which,
HMS Vigilant, was visible from the road. By this time, the narrator recalled,
Robinson 'was beginning to act strangely ... On the evening of 23 October, he
told me he was going out to steal a piece of equipment from one of the Saudi
Arabian Tornados'.[12]

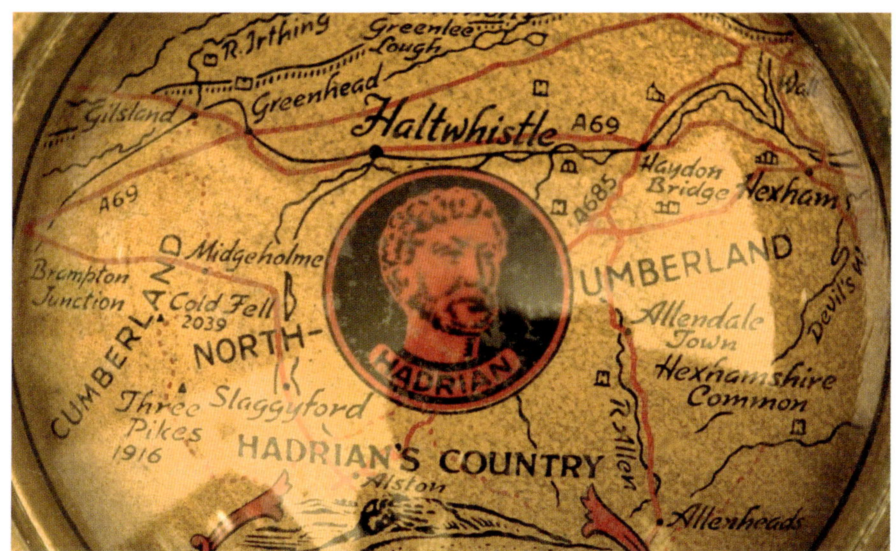

Soon afterwards, having arrived in Northumberland, after visits to Blackpool, Barrow, and Sellafield, 'On 30 October, without warning, we were told that our contracts had been terminated, and we heard on the radio that a Tornado had crashed in the North Sea'.[13]

The narrator's last words, accompanying an image of Hadrian's Wall, are: 'I cannot tell you where Robinson finally found his utopia',[14] followed by a sequence of details of neolithic rock carvings, also in Northumberland, with the sound of meadow pipits calling, and the view along the Tyne in Newcastle, accompanied by Allan Gray's music for Powell and Pressburger's *A Matter of Life and Death*, so that one might infer that utopia, if anywhere, was not far away.

Patrick Keiller
Paperweight with a Map of
Hadrian's Wall 2012

12. *Robinson in Space*, pp.182, 185.
13. Ibid., p.199.
14. Ibid., p.203.

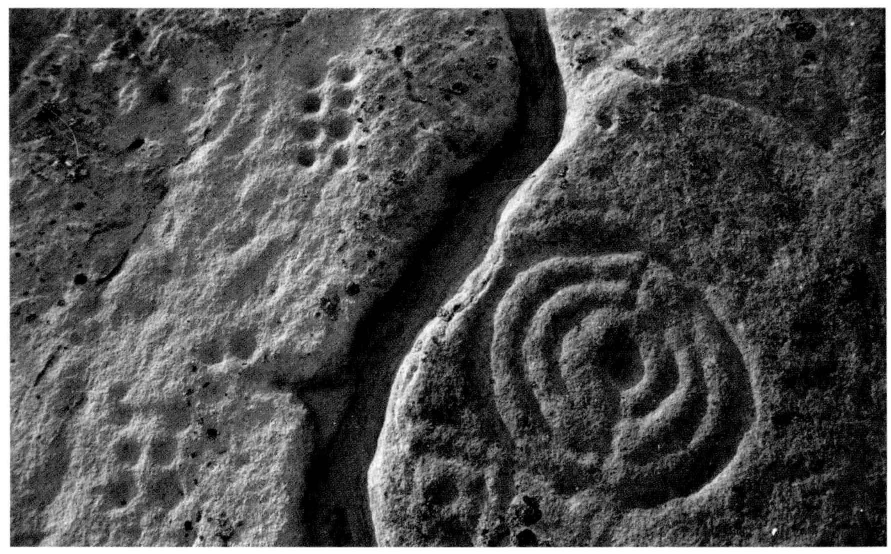

Rock art comprising more or less complex arrangements of concentric circles and other characteristic motifs has been found at a variety of locations in Europe, mostly along or near Atlantic coasts. The motifs are similar to those of some other prehistoric art and the art of some present-day, mostly hunter-gatherer peoples elsewhere in the world, and resemble entoptic forms, characteristic of the early stages of trance experience. In Britain, most examples of rock art are located in northern England and Scotland; they were made between 6,000 and 3,500 years ago, and their meaning and purpose are thought to have been at least partly topographical. In Northumberland, the larger examples are on horizontal or gently sloping surfaces of rock outcrops and large boulders, often near, though not at, the highest points of places overlooking panoramic views, many of these being intervisible locations around the Milfield Basin, near Wooler, about 75 km north of Newcastle.

The presence of so many outstanding examples of this kind of art in the UK is very encouraging: rock art is abstract, international in its distribution (while also, in the UK, oppositionally northern); it was made by people

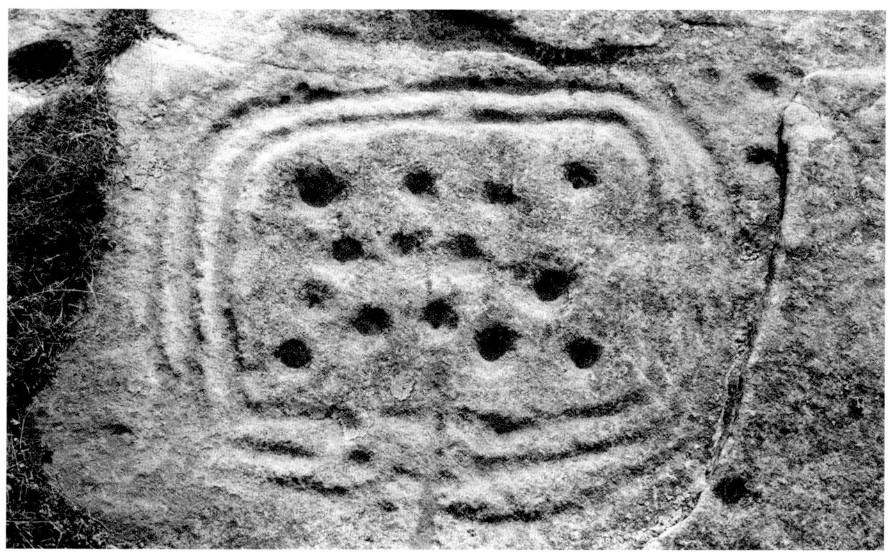

who were mobile, and though they probably moved around within what we would consider a relatively small area – rock art has distinct local characteristics – it demonstrates a way of inhabiting landscape very different to that derived from long-term, essentially agricultural settlement, and the systems of landowning that have been developed from it during recent centuries.

Writing about rock art, the archaeologist Richard Bradley refers to a distinction between the tenure exercised by settled farmers, 'a stable pattern of settlements, boundaries and fields, not unlike the world we inhabit today', and that of hunter-gatherers and other mobile peoples, based on 'paths, places and viewpoints'. Rock art was more significant in the latter context, and 'lost much of its impact as this was replaced by a territorial system depending on stable, mixed farming ... Only then could territories be conceived in terms of an enclosed area and a continuous boundary.'[15] If one seeks instead to reconcile *dwelling* with mobility, the landscapes of rock art might suggest utopian possibilities; and a territory conceived in terms of paths, places and viewpoints sounds very like the landscape of itinerant cinematography.

Patrick Keiller
Details of rock art,
Northumberland 1989

15. Richard Bradley, *Rock Art and the Prehistory of Atlantic Europe: Signing the Land*, London 1997, pp.5, 7.

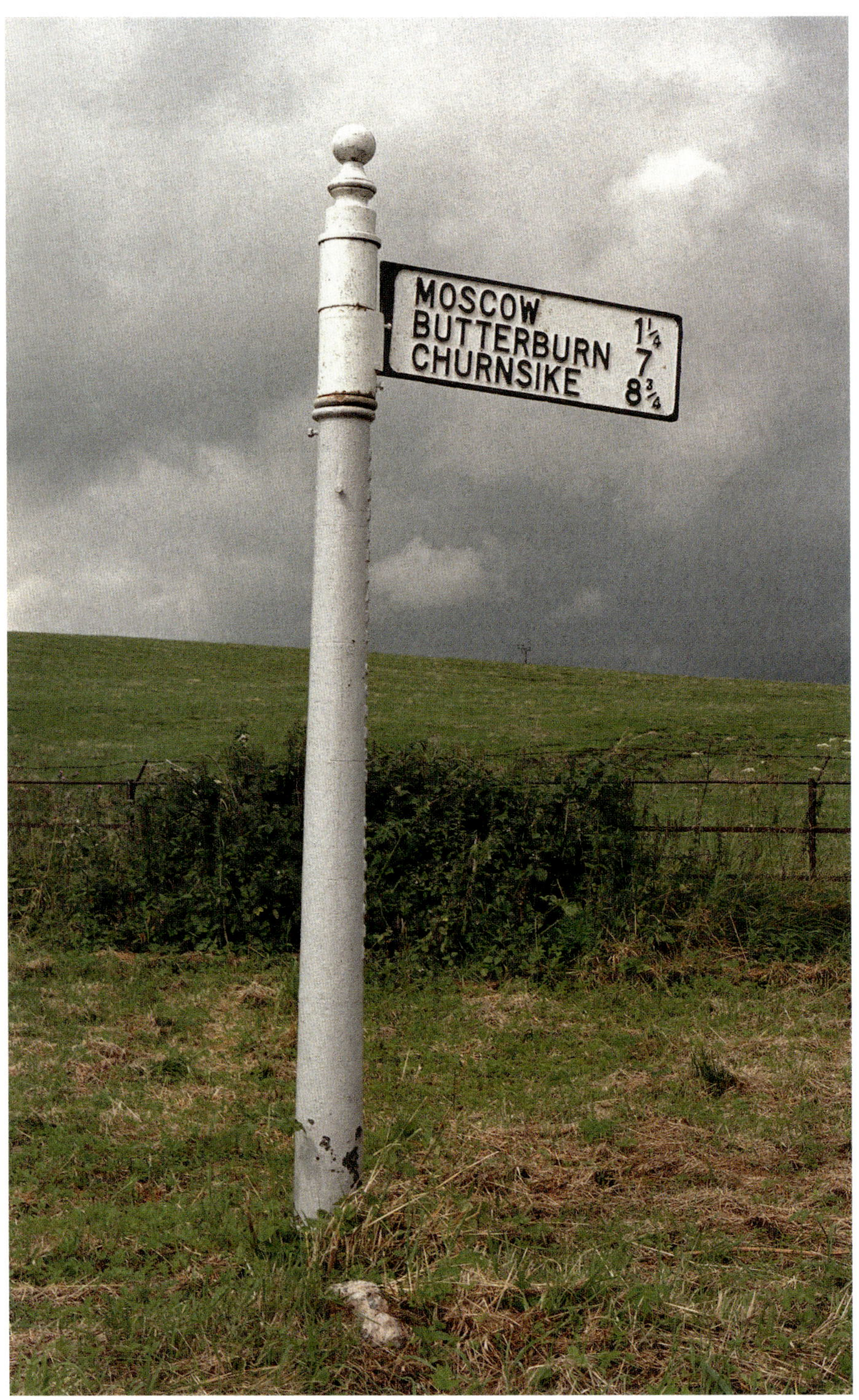

MOSCOW 1¼
BUTTERBURN 7
CHURNSIKE 8¾

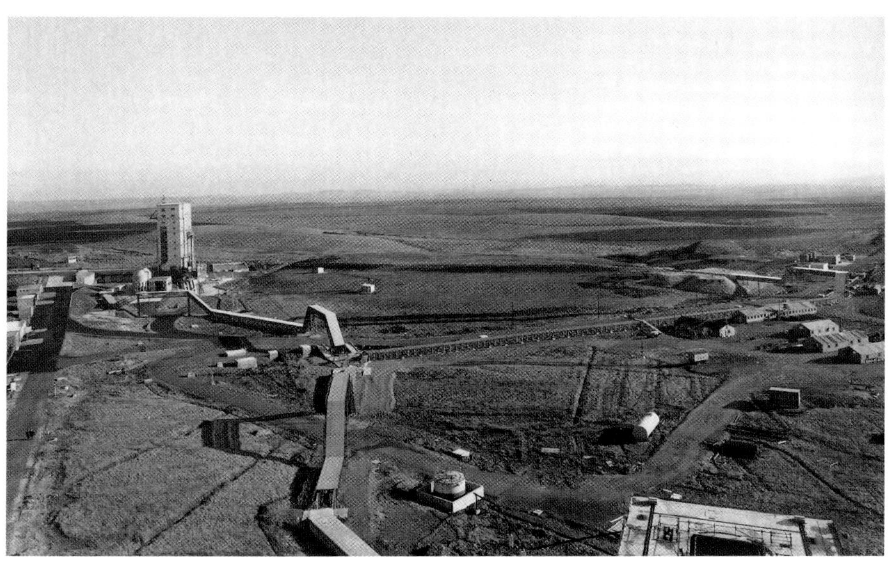

Between 1999, when the book of *Robinson in Space* was published, and 2005, when I began to develop the project that eventually produced *Robinson in Ruins*, I imagined that although Northumberland's rock art may have led him to something like utopia, at a location his former companion felt unable to disclose, Robinson had not stayed there very long; a few days later, he was arrested by Ministry of Defence police, wandering near the UK's Electronic Warfare Tactics Range on Spadeadam Waste in Cumbria, a site first developed for military purposes in the mid-1950s. Spadeadam Waste is one of the border mires, ancient blanket peat bogs covering large parts of the area between Hadrian's Wall and the England-Scotland border.

In 1955, the UK's Ministry of Works designated fifteen square miles of Spadeadam Waste for the construction of the Spadeadam Rocket Establishment, a facility for testing the Rolls-Royce RZ2 rocket engines that were to power the Blue Streak intermediate range ballistic missile, and for carrying out test firings of tethered rockets before they were shipped to the Woomera range in Australia for test launching.

Patrick Keiller, Signpost near
RAF Spadeadam 1987

Spadeadam Rocket Establishment:
rocket test area, c.1960

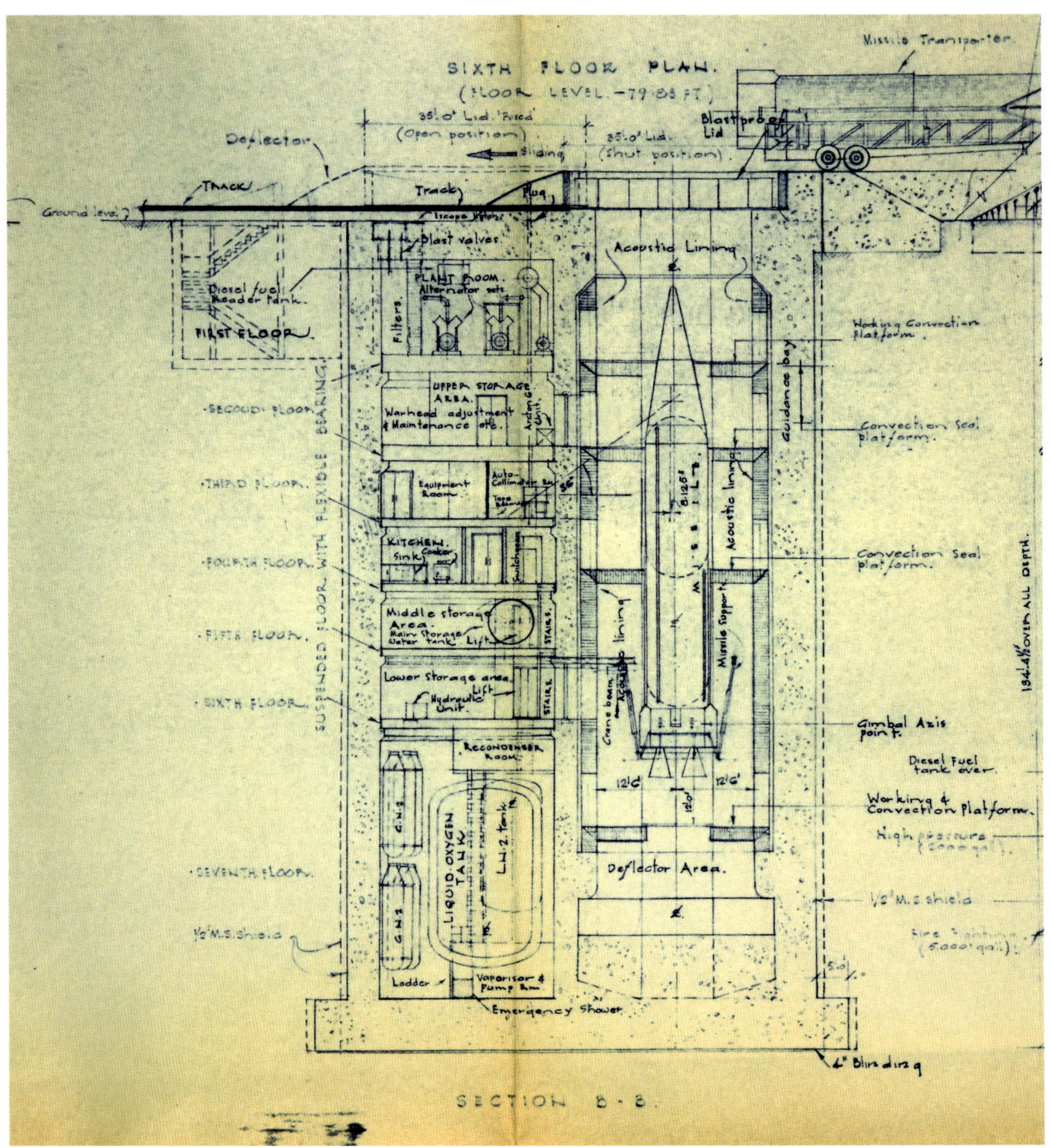
Missile Transporter.
SIXTH FLOOR PLAN.
(FLOOR LEVEL -79.88 FT)
35'.0" Lid 'Fixed' (Open position)
35'.0" Lid. (Shut position)
Blastproof Lid
Deflector.
TRACK
Track
Plug
Ground level
Blast valves
Acoustic Lining
Diesel fuel Header Tank.
PLANT ROOM. Alternator sets
FIRST FLOOR.
Filters.
Working Convection Platform.
Guidance bay
SECOND FLOOR.
UPPER STORAGE AREA.
Warhead adjustment & Maintenance etc.
Antenna Unit.
Convection Seal Platform.
THIRD FLOOR.
Equipment Room.
Auto-Collimator Eye
Acoustic lining
Test
MISSILE 6.125'
FOURTH FLOOR.
KITCHEN.
Sink Cooker
Switchgear
Convection Seal Platform.
FIFTH FLOOR.
Middle storage Area.
Main Storage Water Tank. Lift
STAIRS.
Acoustic lining
Missile Support.
SIXTH FLOOR.
Lower Storage area Lift
Hydraulic Unit.
STAIRS.
Crane beam
Gimbal Axis point.
RECONDENSER ROOM.
12'6"
12'6"
Diesel Fuel tank over.
Working & Convection Platform.
High pressure (5000 gal.)
SEVENTH FLOOR.
G.N.2
LIQUID OXYGEN TANK
L.H.2 tank
12'0"
Deflector Area.
½" M.S shield
½"M.S.shield
G.N.2
Fire fighting (5.000 gal.)
Ladder
Vaporisor & Pump Rm.
Emergency Shower
5'0"
4" Blinding
SECTION B-B.
134.4' OVER ALL DEPTH.
SUSPENDED FLOOR WITH FLEXIBLE BEARING.

It was known at the time that the site was being developed for a military rocket-related purpose, but details of the project were secret. Construction of a trial underground launcher, or silo, began later, but it was not completed, and had been almost forgotten when the unfinished works were exposed by tree felling over forty years later, and surveyed as part of English Heritage's archaeological survey of the Rocket Establishment, in 2004.

Blue Streak's development as a weapon was cancelled in 1960. The decision was taken, supposedly, because of the missile's escalating cost, and the time required to prepare it for launching in the event of incoming attack. The rocket survived as the first stage of the European ELDO satellite launcher, but this too was cancelled in 1972. The US-UK Mutual Defence Agreement had been signed in 1958,[16] and Blue Streak's immediate successor as the future delivery system for the UK's nuclear weapons was the US's air-launched Skybolt, but the US government decided to cancel this in 1962. At a meeting between John F. Kennedy and Harold Macmillan in December 1962 at Nassau in the Bahamas, it was agreed that the UK would buy Polaris missiles, under the terms later set out in the 1963 Polaris Sales Agreement, to be fitted with UK warheads and carried on British-built nuclear submarines. At the time, this was seen as a great bargain, and has since been followed by a similar arrangement for Trident. The terms of supply were such that the UK's missiles became part of a multi-lateral force within NATO, and could be used independently only in situations of extreme national emergency. It has often been pointed out that, since the 1960s, the UK's strategic nuclear weapons have not been credibly independent, and that as a consequence of this and other military dependences, the UK is so constrained in its foreign and other policies that it is, in effect, a US client state.[17]

Design drawing for Blue Streak underground launcher 1959

16. The Agreement between the Government of the United Kingdom of Great Britain and Northern Ireland and the Government of the United States of America for Co-operation on the Uses of Atomic Energy for Mutual Defence Purposes came into force on 4 August 1958. It was renewed most recently in 2004, until 2014.

17. See, for examples, David Leigh and Richard Norton-Taylor, 'We are now a client state', *Guardian*, 17 July 2003; Dan Plesch, *The Future of Britain's WMD*, London 2006; Dan Plesch, 'Let's clear away the Trident delusion', *Independent on Sunday*, 19 September 2010.

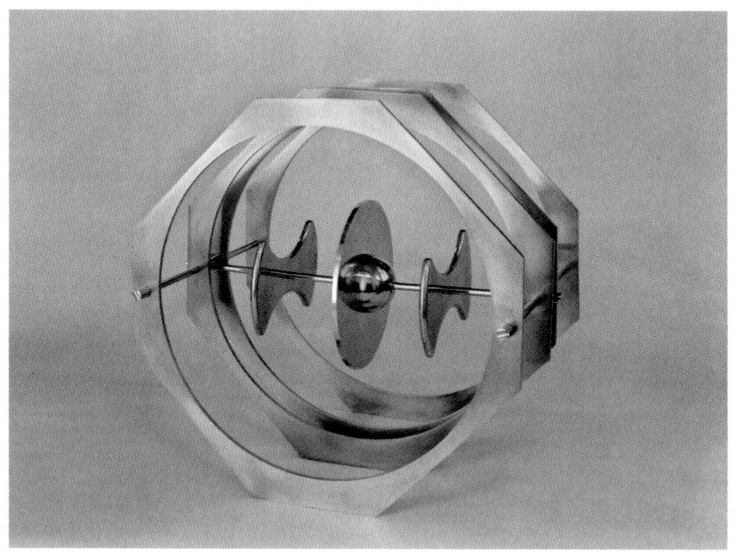

Quatermass II was the second of Nigel Kneale's BBC *Quatermass* television series, broadcast in six episodes at 8 o'clock on Saturday nights in October and November 1955. It was adapted for the cinema as *Quatermass 2*, a feature film produced by Hammer Films, released in 1957.[18] In both versions, Professor Bernard Quatermass is the director of a team developing a nuclear-powered rocket with the aim of establishing permanent bases on the moon. His project is under threat of cancellation by a seemingly cost-conscious government, following a nuclear accident at the rocket project's testing range in Australia. At another UK location, 'Winnerden Flats', meteorite-like projectiles have been falling close to the site of another government research establishment, supposedly developing the production of synthetic food. Anyone who picks up one of the fallen projectiles is liable to be taken over by an alien life-form, briefly visible as an ectoplasm-like sliver when the projectile shatters, which leaves a mark at the point it enters the host, usually on the face. Most of the civil servants in the relevant ministry have already succumbed, so that Quatermass's efforts to reveal and repel the invasion are, initially, frustrated. In both the television series and the film, the Shell Haven refinery near Stanford-le-Hope in Essex, on the Thames estuary, represents the synthetic food establishment, inside which is an enormous, malevolent organism. In the film, the location that represents the temporary settlement where the research establishment's not yet body-snatched but compliant construction workers live was at or near the new town Hemel Hempstead,

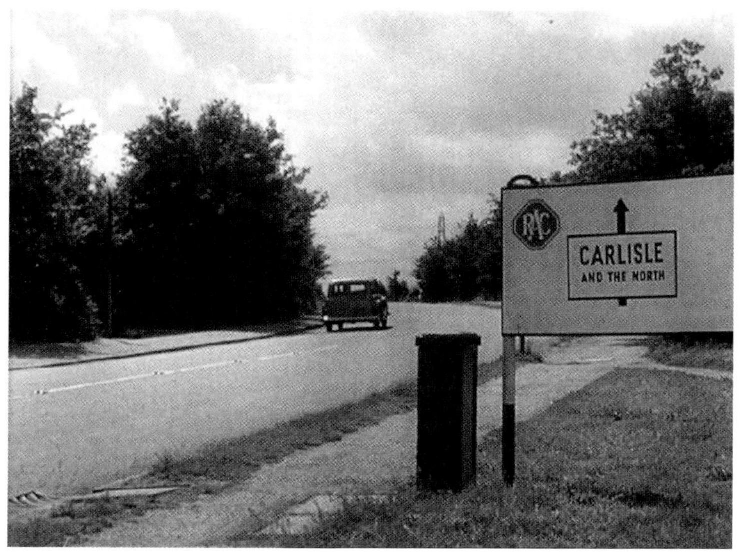

then under construction. Early in the Hammer film, Quatermass and a colleague set out from the rocket base to drive to Winnerden Flats. In the car, the colleague reads a map, telling Quatermass: 'You take the Carlisle road'. Turning off what appears to be a recently constructed road, perhaps somewhere in Essex, or Hemel Hempstead, they pass a sign 'Carlisle and the North', put there, presumably, by the film crew. There had been no mention of Carlisle, about twenty miles from Spadeadam, in the original television series.

Given the effort and expense involved, one wonders why these set-ups were added to the story already established by the television series. Perhaps they were intended merely to associate Quatermass's fictional rocket site with the actual test facility that would have been known, by the time of the film, to be under construction. More recently, since the controversy over Trident has exposed the realities of the UK's nuclear weapons predicament, *Quatermass 2*'s allusion

Bryan Kneale
Marina 1967

Frame from *Quatermass 2* (1957)

18. The first and third series were *The Quatermass Experiment*, broadcast in six episodes (of which only two survive) on Saturday evenings between 18 July and 22 August 1953 and *Quatermass and the Pit*, broadcast in six episodes on Monday nights between 22 December 1958 and 26 January 1959. By the end of the latter, BBC audience research indicated 11 million viewers. Hammer also produced feature-film adaptations of these series: *The Quatermass Xperiment* (1955) and *Quatermass and the Pit* (1967).

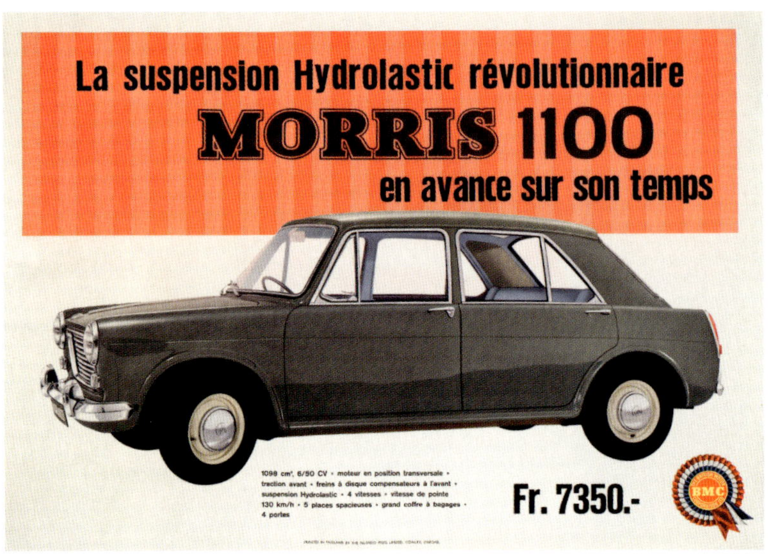

to Spadeadam has suggested a more specific interpretation: for Robinson
the former Rocket Establishment was associated with the loss of the UK's
strategic independence in the period since Blue Streak's cancellation, which
he attributed to the take-over of the UK by a malevolent intelligence like those
envisaged in *Quatermass II/2* and *Invasion of the Body Snatchers*. This was,
perhaps, a manifestation of the *Great Malady* that he would set out to dispel
on his release from prison: the decision to purchase Polaris led to the French
veto, in 1963, of the UK's 1960 application to join the European Economic
Community, which impacted so severely on the UK's manufacturing
industry by denying it tariff-free access to what would have been the largest
market for its exports.[19]

19. See, for example, Karel Williams, Colin Haslam, Sukhdev Johal, John
Williams, with Andy Adcroft, *Cars: Analysis, History, Cases*, Providence 1994,
pp.134–65: BMC's 1100 was launched in 1962 as a 'world car'; although it was
the UK's biggest-selling design for most of the decade, its export was severely
restricted by the UK's failure to join the European Economic Community.

**Morris 1100 poster produced for
the Swiss market, c.1962**

Robinson in Ruins:
**K2 rocket motor test structure,
Westcott Venture Park**

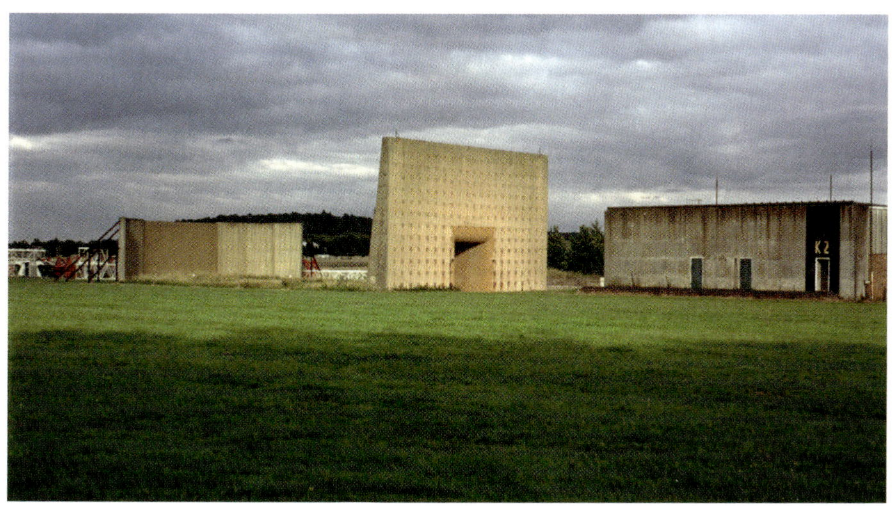

In January 2008, Robinson was released from a fictional open prison at Edgcott in Buckinghamshire, which is near two real prisons and, coincidentally, the former RAF Westcott, where the Rocket Propulsion Establishment was set up in 1946. This is another site where Blue Streak's RZ2 motors were tested, now the Westcott Venture Park, where rocketry continues.

On the pages that follow, text in grey is quoted from the narration of *Robinson in Ruins*.

Patrick Keiller
Montage of details of lichen on
road sign 2008–11
'He believed that he could
communicate with a network of
non-human intelligences ... They
were determined to preserve the
possibility of life's survival on the
planet, and enlisted him to work
on their behalf.'
' ... To begin with, he thought the
profile might be that of Goethe
or, perhaps, one of the Berkshire
magistrates.'

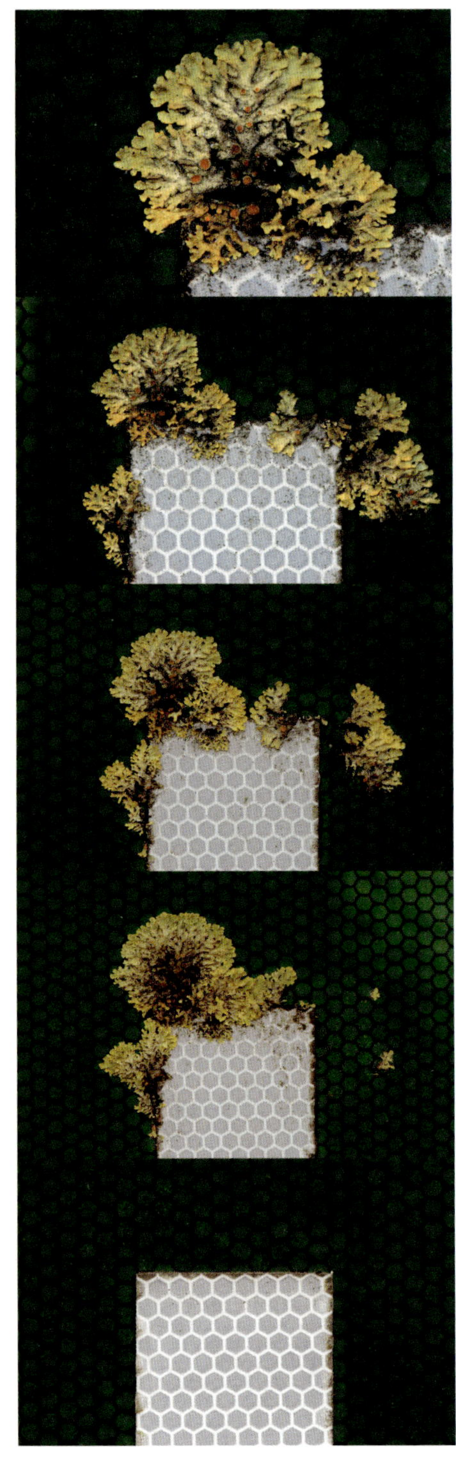

1795

On the city's outskirts, Robinson encountered his first *picturesque view*: a road sign, colonised by the lichen *Xanthoria Parietina*, which he understood to mean that he should set out for Newbury.

He had read that one of the factors that enabled industrial capitalism to develop first in England was the mobility of the previously settled agricultural workforce. Such labour-market flexibility, however, derived not from any Anglo-Saxon, customary freedoms, but from government legislation: *An Act to prevent the Removal of Poor Persons until they shall actually become chargeable*, the 1795 amendment to the Settlement Act 'in the interest of freeing hands to go where burgeoning capitalist enterprise needed them most'.[20]

That same year, a meteorite fell in Yorkshire, which confirmed the reality of meteorites, and led Robinson to conclude that a meteorite fall necessarily coincides with an event of major historical significance.

in the eighth and ninth years
of the reign of King William.

3. the third intituled "an act for
"supplying some defects in the laws
"for the relief of the poor of this
"kingdom" hath been found very
ineffectual and it is necessary
that other provisions should be
made relating thereto Be it there-
fore ENACTED by the King's most
excellent Majesty by and with the
advice and consent of the Lords
spiritual and temporal and
Commons in this present parliament assembled and by the
authority of the same that from
and after the passing of this act
so much of the said in part recited
act of the thirteenth and fourteenth
years of King Charles the second
as enables the justices to remove
any person or persons that are
likely to be chargeable to the
parish township or place into
which they shall come to inhabit
shall be and the same is hereby
repealed and that from thenceforth
no poor person shall be removed
by virtue of any order of removal
from the parish or place where
such poor person shall be inhabiting to the place of his or her
last legal settlement until such
person shall have become actually
chargeable to the parish township
or place in which such person
shall then inhabit in which case
two justices of the peace are hereby
impowered to remove the person
or persons in the same manner
and subject to the same appeal
and with the same powers as

4. might have been done before the
passing of this act with respect
to persons likely to become chargeable ALSO whereas poor persons

An Act to prevent the Removal of Poor Persons until they shall actually become chargeable (35 Geo III c.101) 1795

Patrick Keiller
Monument to meteorite fall, near Wold Newton, Yorkshire 2007. The inscription is:

Here/On this Spot, Decr. 13th. 1795/Fell from the Atmofphere/ AN EXTRAORDINARY STONE/ In Breadth 28 inches/In Length 30 inches/and/Whose Weight was 56 Pounds/THIS COLUMN/ In Memory of it/Was erected by/ EDWARD TOPHAM/1799.

Wold Cottage meteorite (stone, ordinary chondrite) Fragments of the meteorite are preserved in the Natural History Museum. It fell on 13 December 1795, about five hundred metres from Wold Cottage, the house of Edward Topham, near the village of Wold Newton in Yorkshire.

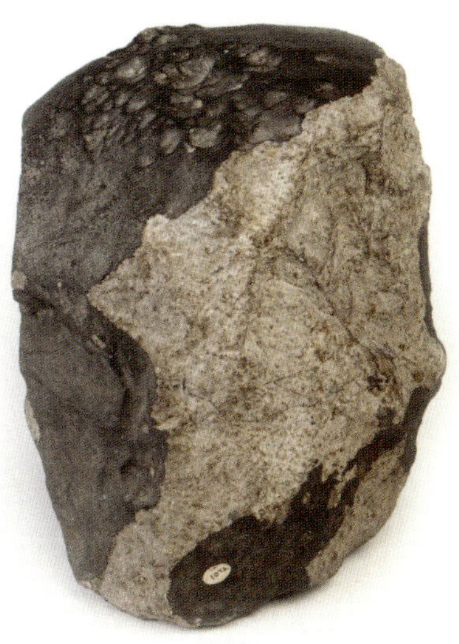

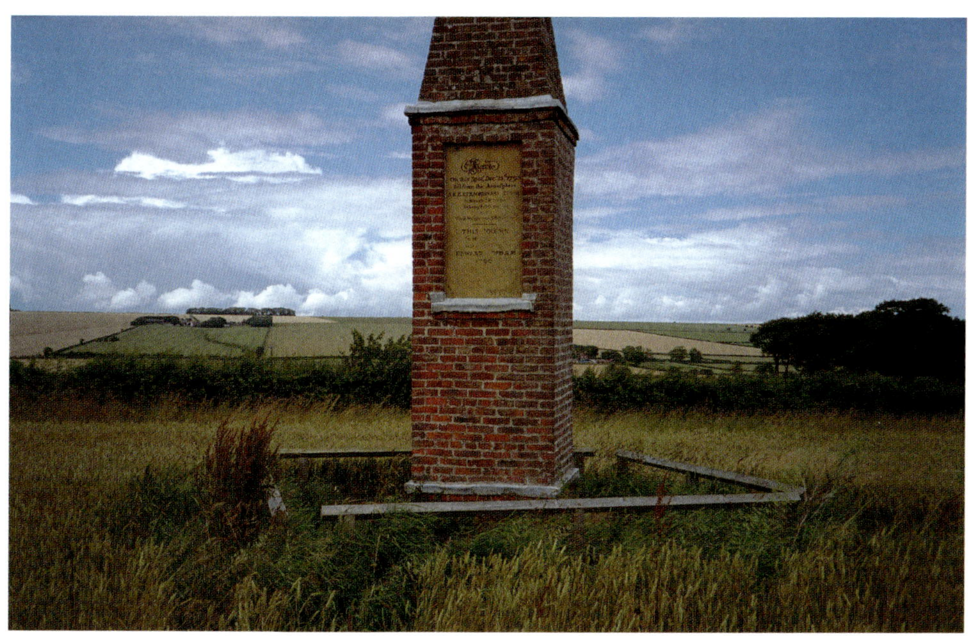

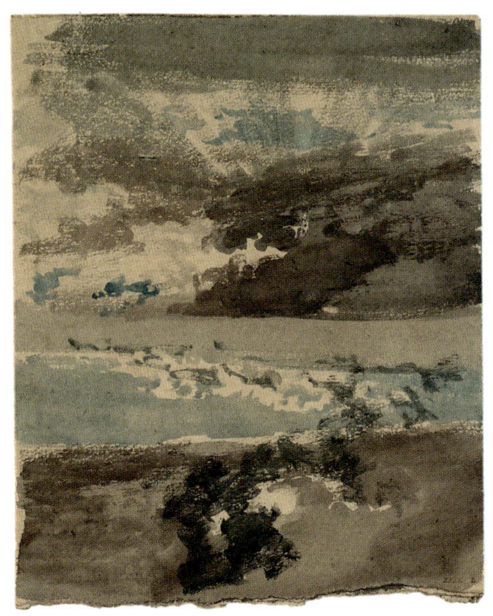

In the Belousov-Zhabotinskii reaction, chemical scroll waves can appear spontaneously or be initiated by touching the surface of the reagent with a hot filament, as in this series of photographs by Fritz Goro, in Ilya Prigogine's *From Being to Becoming: Time and Complexity in the Physical Sciences*, published in 1980.

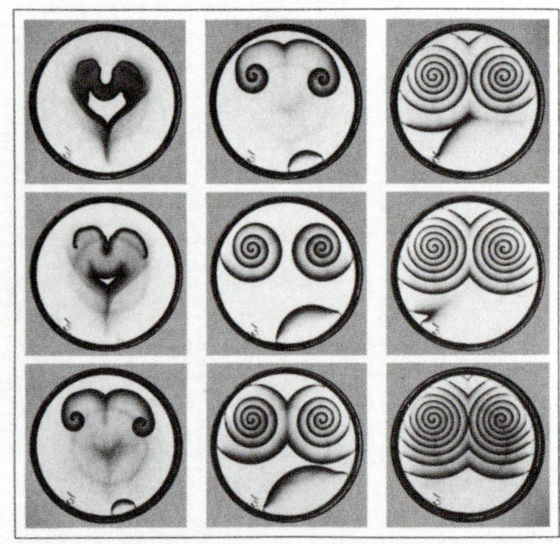

In Marx's doctoral thesis, *The Difference Between the Democritean and Epicurean Philosophy of Nature*, he found Epicurus's theory of meteors, which he understood as a reference to the weather.

In Chapter 5 of Part 2 of the thesis, 'The Meteors', Marx writes that for Epicurus: 'in the meteors everything occurs in a multiple and unregulated way, that everything in them is to be explained by a manifold of indefinitely many causes' and that he 'ascribes to them …

all the anxiety and confusion of men'.

On May 6th, he reached Donnington Castle, on the outskirts of Newbury.

While the Civil War, he read, 'did not create a capitalist society where none had existed before', it was 'a milestone in the evolution of property relations and the state in England'.[21]

He was reading Karl Polanyi's *The Great Transformation*, published in 1944, which

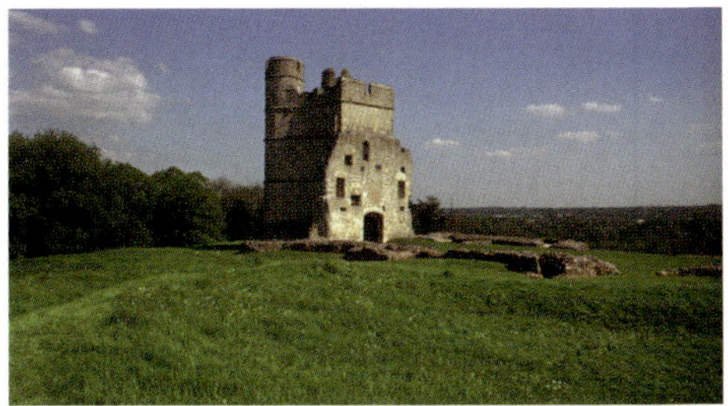

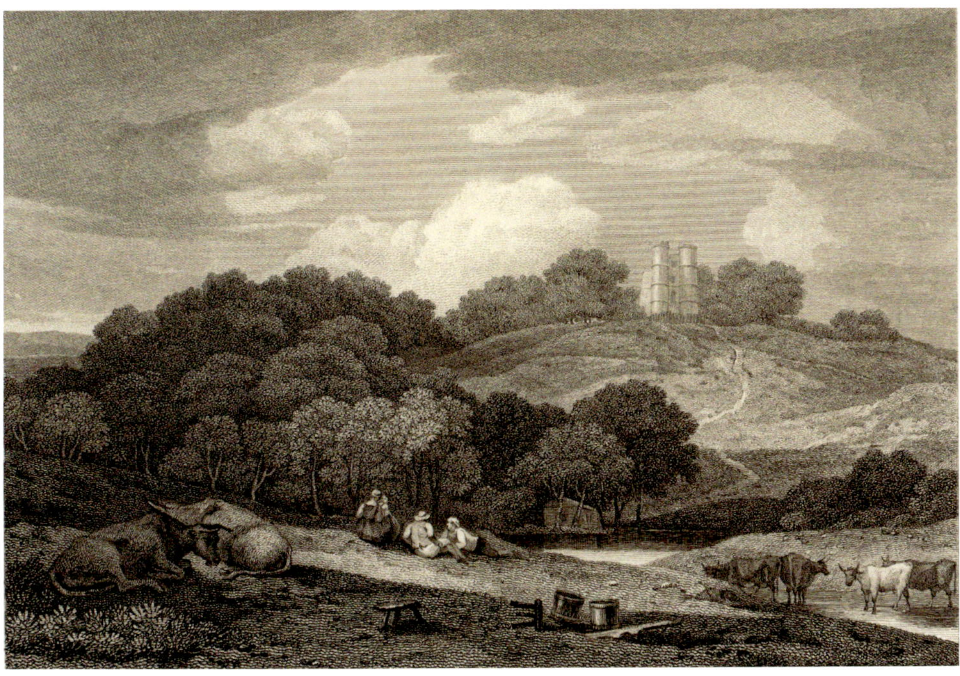

locates the origin of twentieth-century catastrophe in the development of market society in England. Polanyi accorded great significance to the system of poor relief devised by the Berkshire magistrates on 6 May 1795, at the Pelican Inn, in Speenhamland, a part of Newbury. The system guaranteed a minimum income linked to the price of bread, which had risen steeply. It offered landless agricultural workers some protection from the displacement intended by the changes to the Settlement Act.

The Pelican Inn – the George and Pelican, as it was in 1795 – was a large coaching inn on the road from London to Bristol, later a bank. There was no sign of its having been the site of any historic decision.

The system devised at Speenhamland was denounced by market liberals and others, including Edmund Burke who, in 1795, wrote in *Thoughts and Details on Scarcity* that:

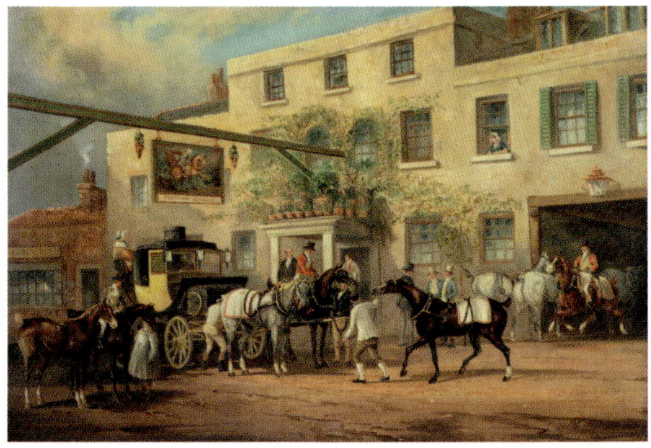

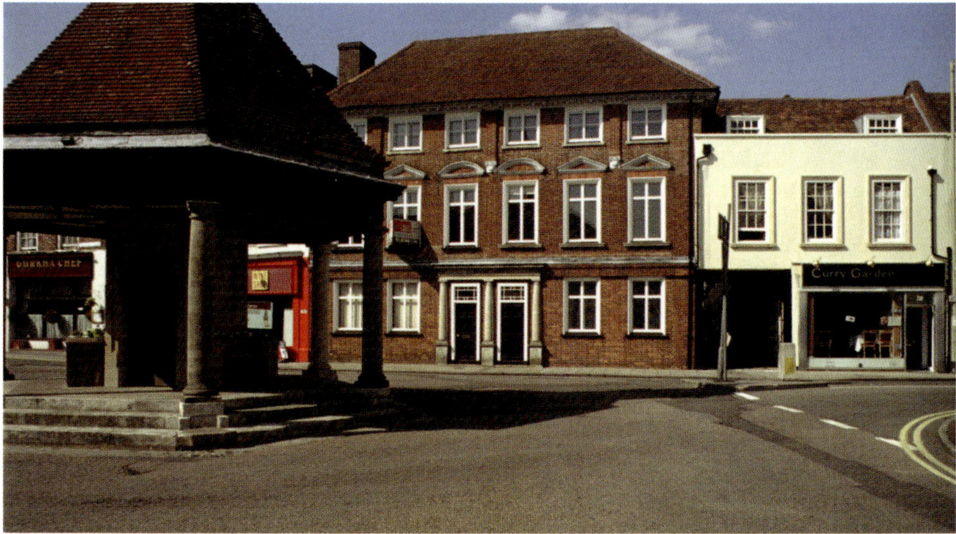

'We, the people, ought to be made sensible, that it is not in breaking the laws of commerce, which are the laws of nature, and consequently the laws of God, that we are to place our hope of softening the Divine displeasure to remove any calamity under which we suffer, or which hangs over us.'[22]

Polanyi argued that *laissez-faire* was planned, whereas Speenhamland was society's spontaneous reaction to the disasters that were accompanying its imposition. 'The idea of a self-adjusting market', he wrote, 'implied a stark utopia. Such an institution could not exist for any length of time without annihilating the human and natural substance of society.'[23]

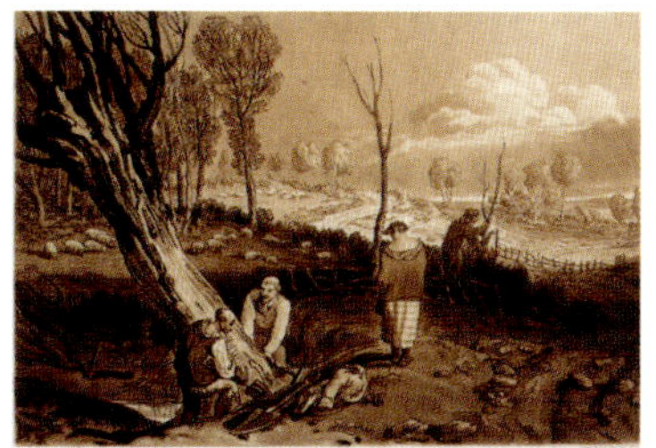

J.M.W. Turner
Hedging and Ditching, engraving
from *The Liber Studiorum* 1812

J.M.W. Turner
Harvest Home 1809

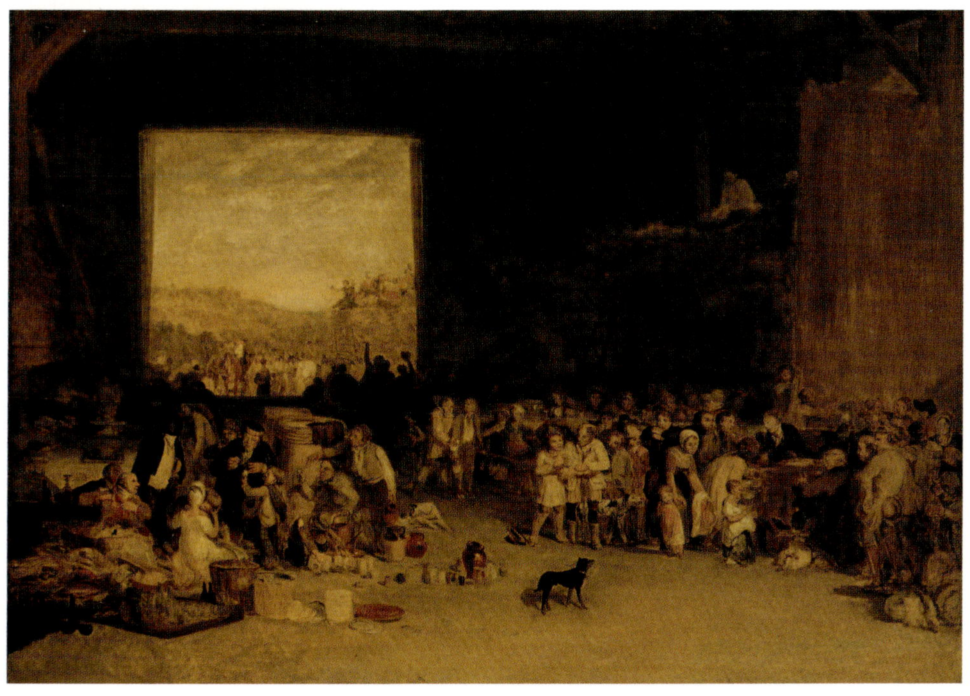

20. John Torpey, *The Invention of the Passport: Surveillance,
Citizenship and the State*, Cambridge 1999, p.67.
21. Ellen Meiksins Wood, *The Pristine Culture of Capitalism*,
London 1991, p.126.
22. Edmund Burke, *Thoughts and Details on Scarcity,
Originally Presented to the Right Hon. William Pitt,
in the Month of November, 1795*, London 1800, p.32.
23. Karl Polanyi, *The Great Transformation:
The Political and Economic Origins of Our Time*,
Boston 1944/2001, p.3.

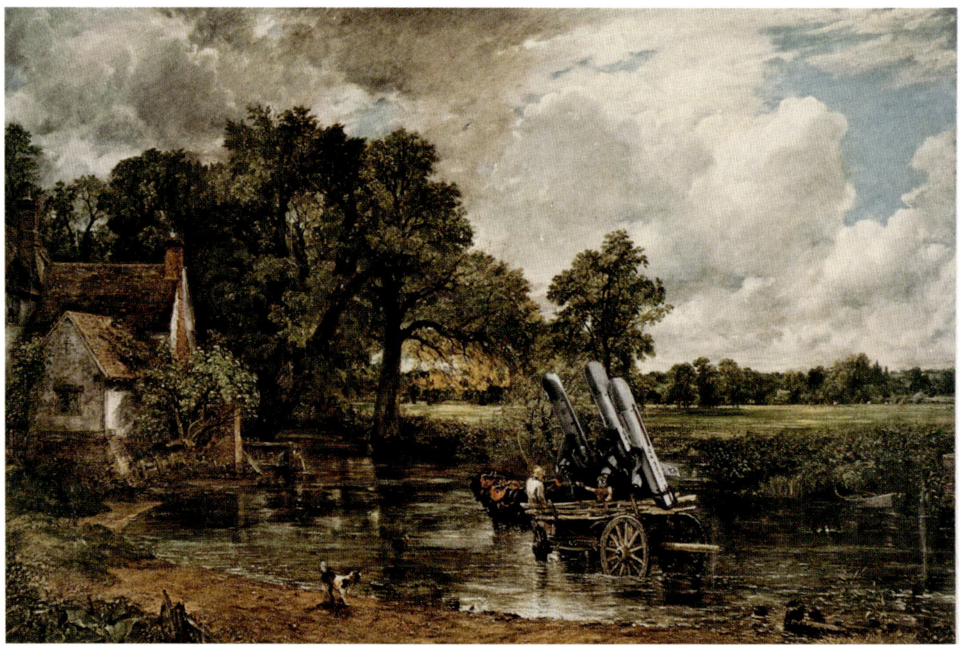

Peter Kennard
Haywain with Cruise Missiles
1980

Greenham Common, Aldermaston and the Government Pipeline and Storage System

Robinson walked on until he came to Greenham Common …

The last cruise missiles in Europe had been removed in March 1991, under the terms of the 1987 INF Treaty. There had been ninety-six Gryphon ground-launched missiles with nuclear warheads at the base.

Greenham was the first US Air Force base in Europe where cruise missiles had been sited. The UK government had announced NATO's decision in June 1980; the Women's Peace Camp began in September of the following year. In 1988, the Peace Camp had established that, since the base's presence infringed commoner's rights, it must have always been illegal.

He had wanted to see the inscription: FAY CE QUE VOULDRAS – 'do what you will', the single rule of Rabelais's ideal community, the Abbey of Thélème. The rule was borrowed from a homily of St Augustine of Hippo: 'Love,

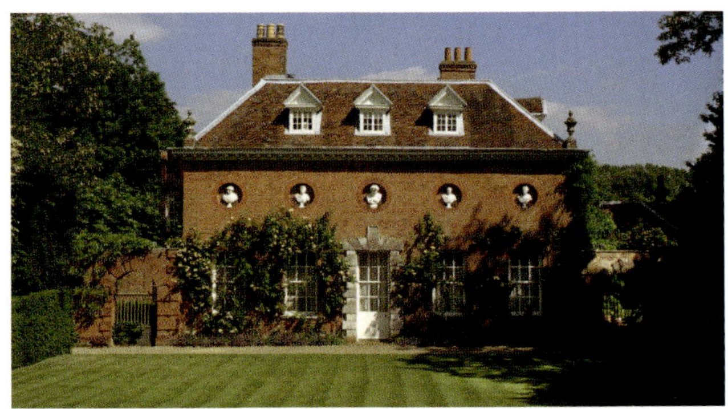

Robinson in Ruins: West Green House, Hampshire

Robinson in Ruins: inscription 'Fay ce que vouldras', West Green House

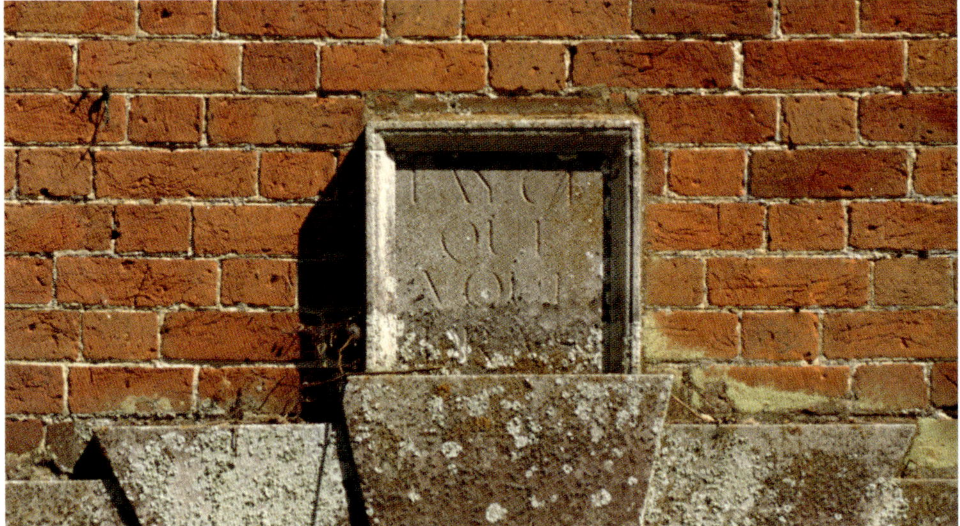

and do what you will.' In the eighteenth century, Rabelais's words were adopted as the motto of the Hell Fire Club, and in the twentieth, by Aleister Crowley. [West Green House] was rebuilt in the eighteenth century by Henry 'Hangman' Hawley, who commanded the cavalry at Culloden. In the 1980s, it had been let to Alistair, Lord McAlpine, treasurer and deputy chairman of Margaret Thatcher's Conservative Party.

Robinson was saddened by these appropriations of Rabelais's ideal community, which he understood to be based on the belief that 'people … have naturally an instinct and spur that prompteth them unto virtuous actions'.

He hung about the neighbourhood for several days, begging in the woods until, eventually, he was sufficiently encouraged to return to Aldermaston.

In 1993, the Atomic Weapons Establishment became a 'Government Owned, Contractor Operated' or *GO-CO* institution. Since 2000,

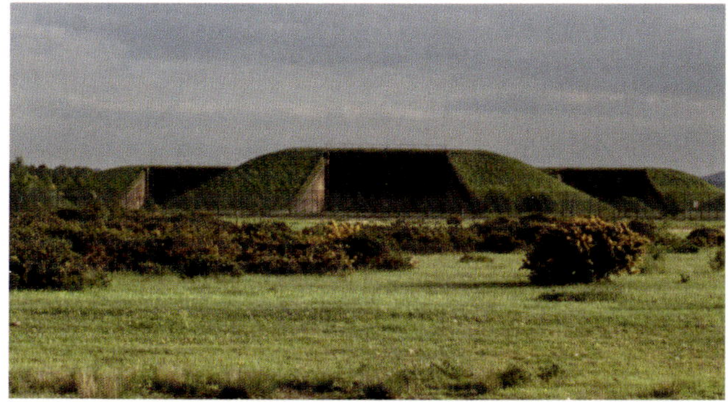

Robinson in Ruins: cruise missile shelters, Greenham Common

Robinson in Ruins: MoD byelaw notice, Atomic Weapons Establishment, Aldermaston

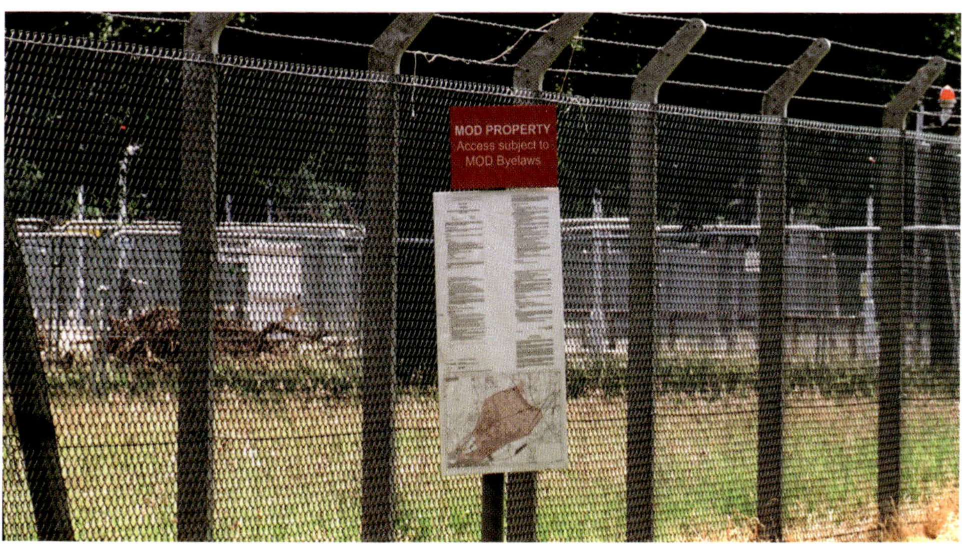

it had been operated by a joint venture of three equal partners: the state-owned British Nuclear Fuels Ltd, Serco, a UK private-sector company with roles in many challenging areas of the public sector, and the US aerospace company Lockheed Martin.

The government later sold its BNFL share to the Jacobs Engineering Group, a US company, so that the UK's nuclear weapons production was in two-thirds US ownership. A few months later, it was reported that the AWE was undertaking work for the US military, both these circumstances being arguably in breach of the Nuclear Non-Proliferation Treaty, which forbids the sharing of nuclear weapons technology by independent states.

At Padworth Common, near Aldermaston, he found another strategic asset: one of the largest depots of the Government Pipeline and Storage System, which supplied aviation and other fuels to US and UK military bases, and the UK's civil airports.

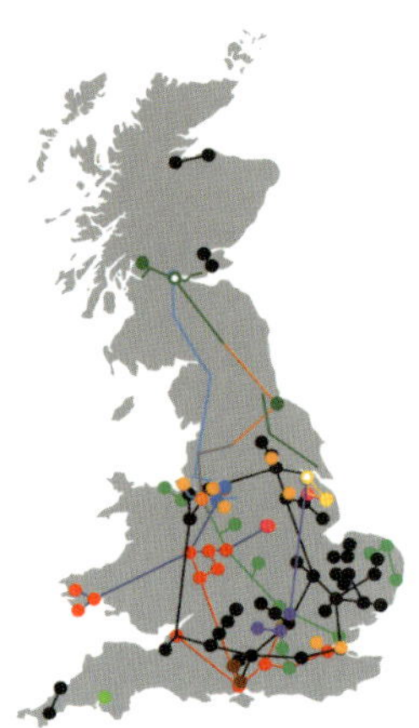

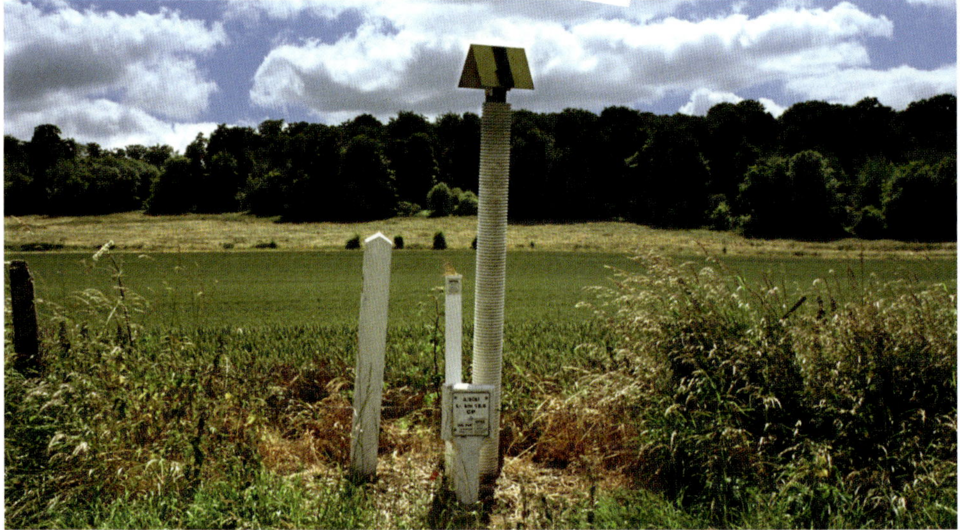

The GPSS was initiated in 1942; it interconnected with the oil companies' networks, and its civil use produced revenue for the Ministry of Defence. The agreement to supply US bases had been renewed most recently in 2004.

The GPSS comprises about 2,500 kilometres of pipeline, and forty-six depots, eleven of which are still in use. It moves about 5 billion litres of fuel every year.

During the Second World War, the GPSS supplied oil to Operation Pluto (Pipe Lines Under The Ocean) developed by Arthur Hartley, Chief Engineer of the Anglo-Iranian Oil Company. On 17 June 1914, the British government had purchased a controlling interest in the Anglo-Persian Oil Company, securing access to a source of oil that supplied the UK during two world wars. Anglo-Persian was the first company to extract petroleum from the Middle East on a commercial scale, set up in 1909; it was renamed the Anglo-

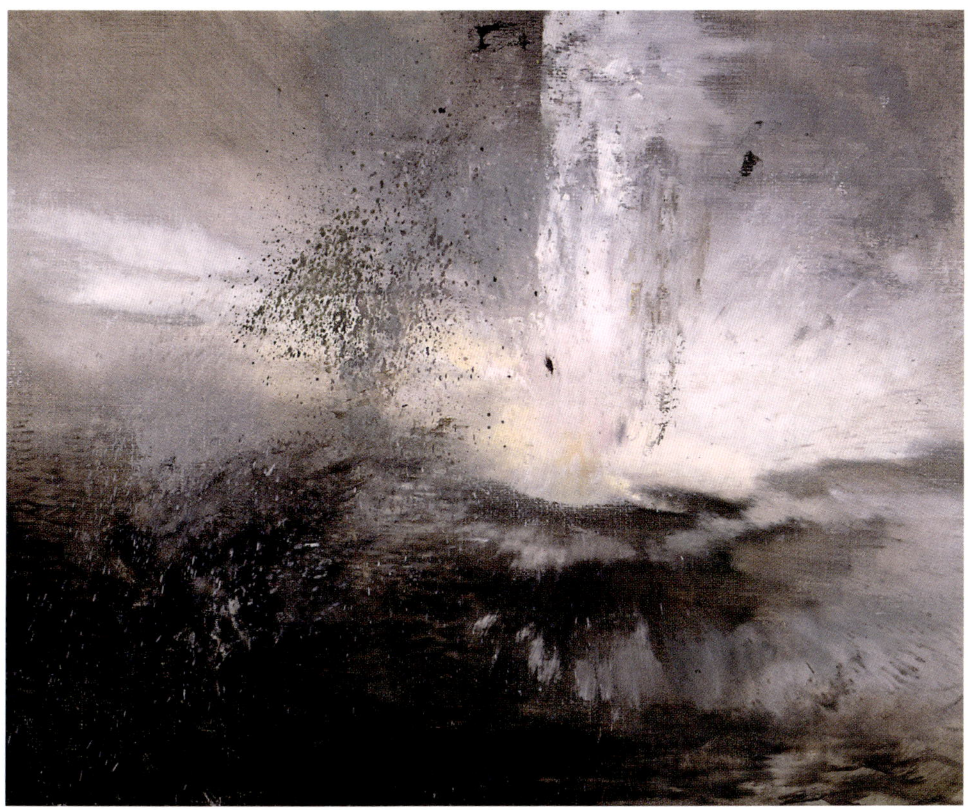

Iranian Oil Company in 1935. In 1951, the
Iranian parliament voted to nationalise the
oil industry, which led in 1953 to the British-
and US-organised coup that installed the
dictatorship of the Shah, itself overthrown,
eventually, by the Iranian revolution in 1979.
In 1954, Anglo-Iranian became the British
Petroleum Company, which is now BP plc.

At a meeting of the Royal Geographical
Society on 11 May 1942, the Society's
secretary delivered a paper:

'In February 1940 the late Lord Lloyd, then
Chairman of the British Council, proposed
to our then President, Field-Marshall Sir
Philip Chetwode, that the Society should
undertake to make a map in Arabic characters
of existing and potential war areas: Europe,
North Africa, and the Middle East up to the
Indian frontier, which he thought would be
of political importance and use in the work
of the British Council.

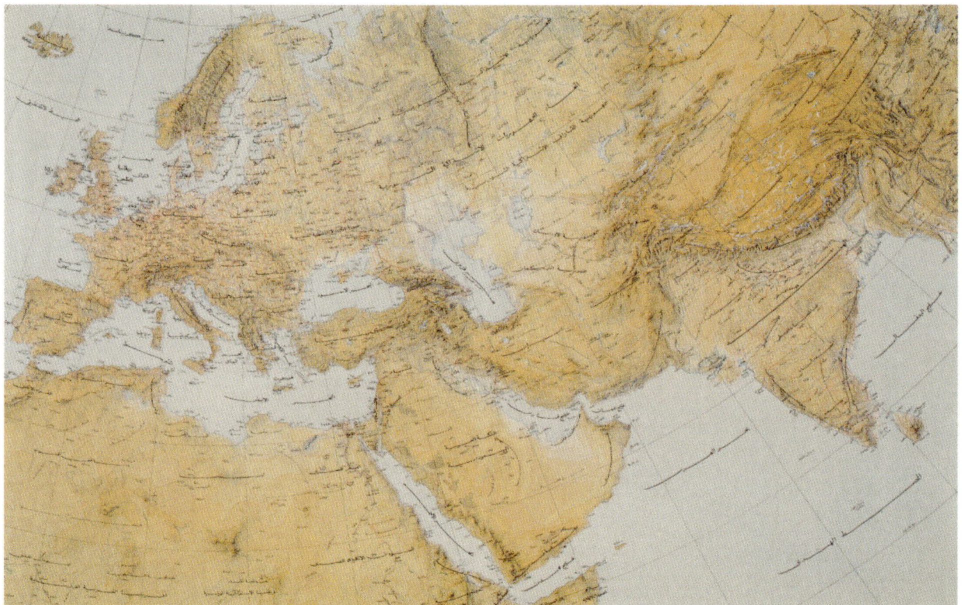

'For a long time the project was, in the files of the British Council, the Arab map, though it soon became evident that as the name plate would be compiled in English, an English edition would naturally be produced at the same time as the Arab; and that if one took care to keep all names and numerals on the black plate, there was nothing to prevent editions in any language or characters.

'... Major oilfields are shown by symbol, as are principal pipelines.'[24]

24. Arthur R Hinks, 'Making the British Council Map', *The Geographical Journal*, vol.100, no.3, September 1942, pp.123–30.

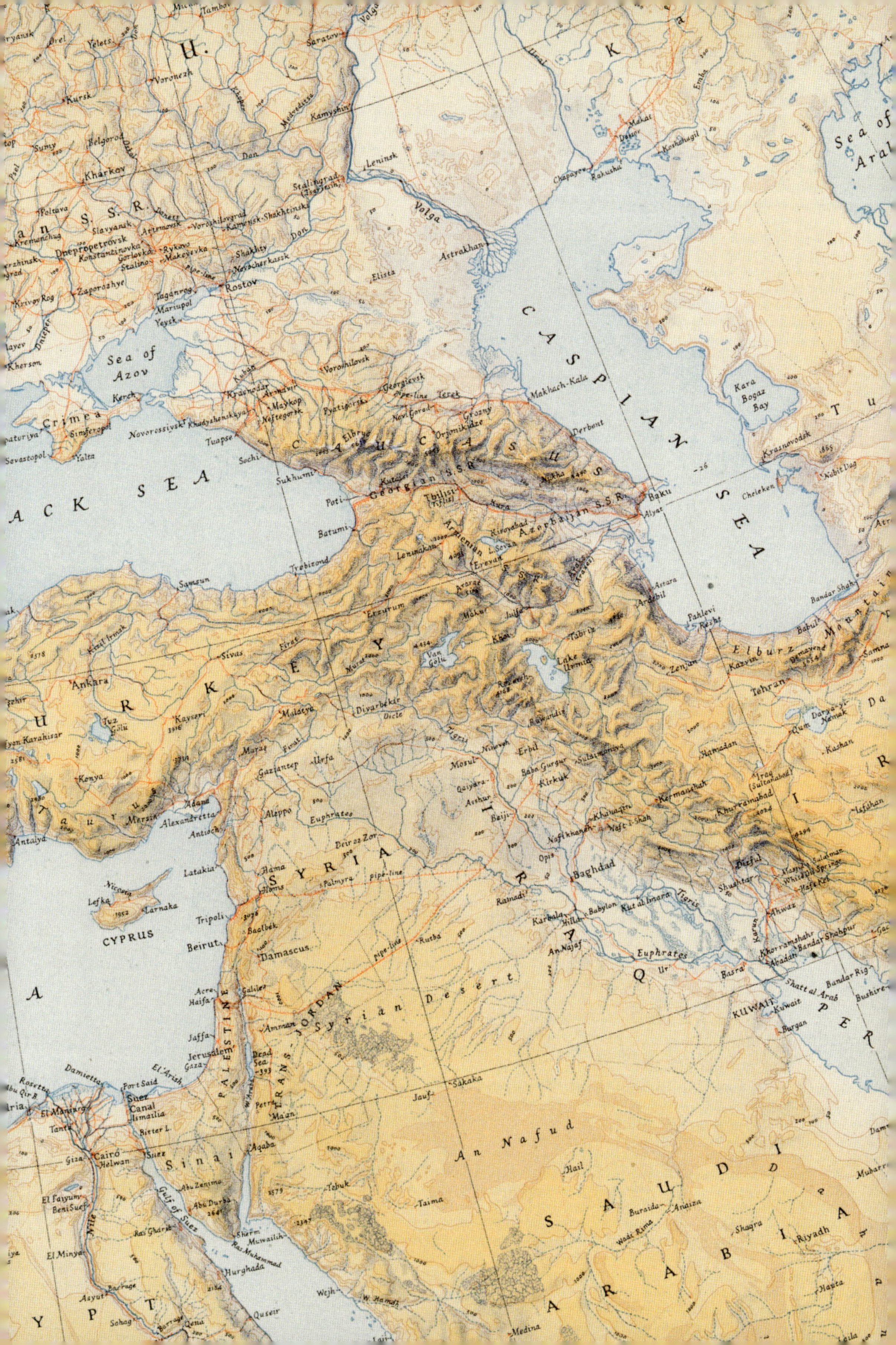

Sea of Aral
CASPIAN SEA
Black Sea
Sea of Azov
Crimea
Kara Bogaz Bay
CAUCASUS
Georgian S.S.R.
Armenian S.S.R.
Azerbaijan S.S.R.
TURKEY
SYRIA
IRAQ
IRAN
CYPRUS
PALESTINE
TRANS-JORDAN
SAUDI ARABIA
Syrian Desert
An Nafud
EGYPT
Sinai
Elburz Mountains
R.S.F.S.R.
U.S.S.R.
Ukrainian S.S.R.
Moscow
Voronezh
Kharkov
Rostov
Stalingrad
Astrakhan
Baku
Tbilisi
Tiflis
Erevan
Ankara
Kayseri
Konya
Sivas
Erzurum
Diyarbekir
Mosul
Kirkuk
Baghdad
Basra
Tehran
Hamadan
Isfahan
Kuwait
Damascus
Beirut
Tripoli
Aleppo
Hama
Homs
Jerusalem
Amman
Haifa
Jaffa
Gaza
Port Said
Suez Canal
Cairo
Helwan
Giza
Medina
Riyadh
Hail
Buraida
Anaiza
Lake Urmia
Van Golu
Euphrates
Tigris
Nile
Gulf of Suez
Gulf of Aqaba
Dead Sea

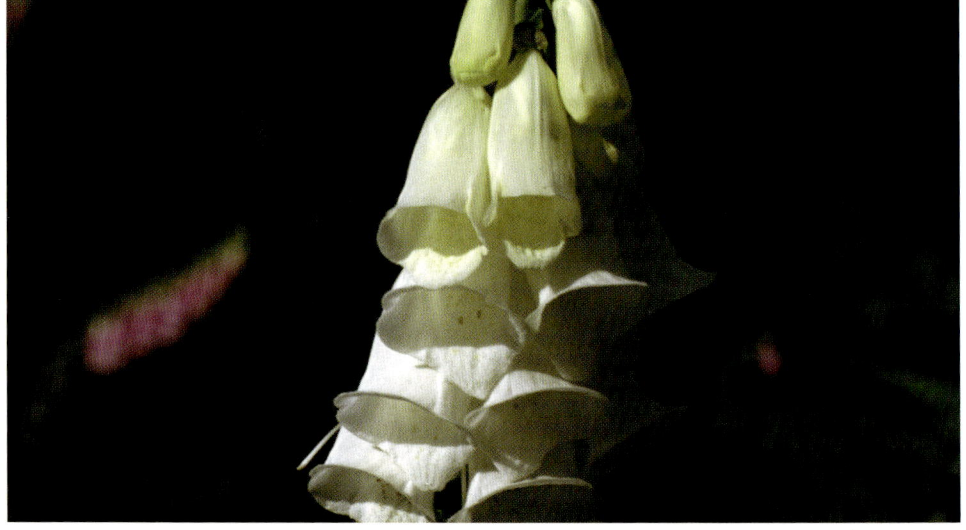

Robinson in Ruins:
foxglove, near Oxford

The non-human,
the post-human

As a surrealist, Robinson believed that designers of artefacts should seek to emulate the morphogenesis of life-forms, and pursued this, and similar questions, in encounters with flowers. He inclined to *biophilia*, the love of life and living systems, having discovered Lynn Margulis's view that symbiotic relationships between organisms, often of different phyla, are a primary force in evolution. He was inspired by her endorsement of the Russian botanists who had formulated the theory in the 1920s, and by her denunciation of neo-Darwinism, and all 'capitalistic, competitive, cost-benefit' interpretations of Darwin.

In the journal *Nature*, it was argued that rates of species extinction had been seriously under-estimated. Four years earlier, a forty-year study of plants, birds and, in particular, butterflies in Britain, had given a firm indication of approaching mass-extinction.

There were several anticipated scenarios: in one, within two or three hundred years,

Barbara Hepworth
Sun and Moon 1969

John Latham
Full Stop 1961

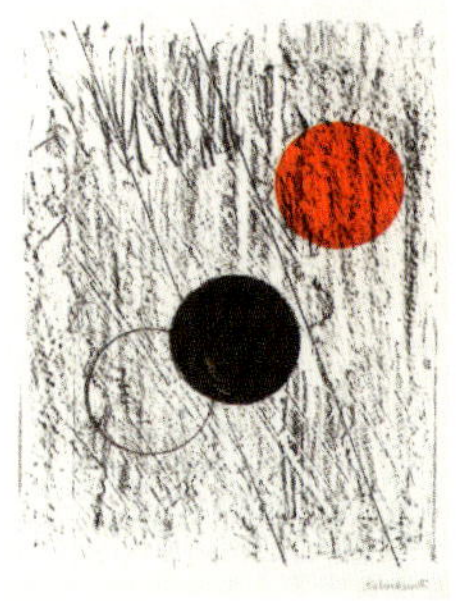

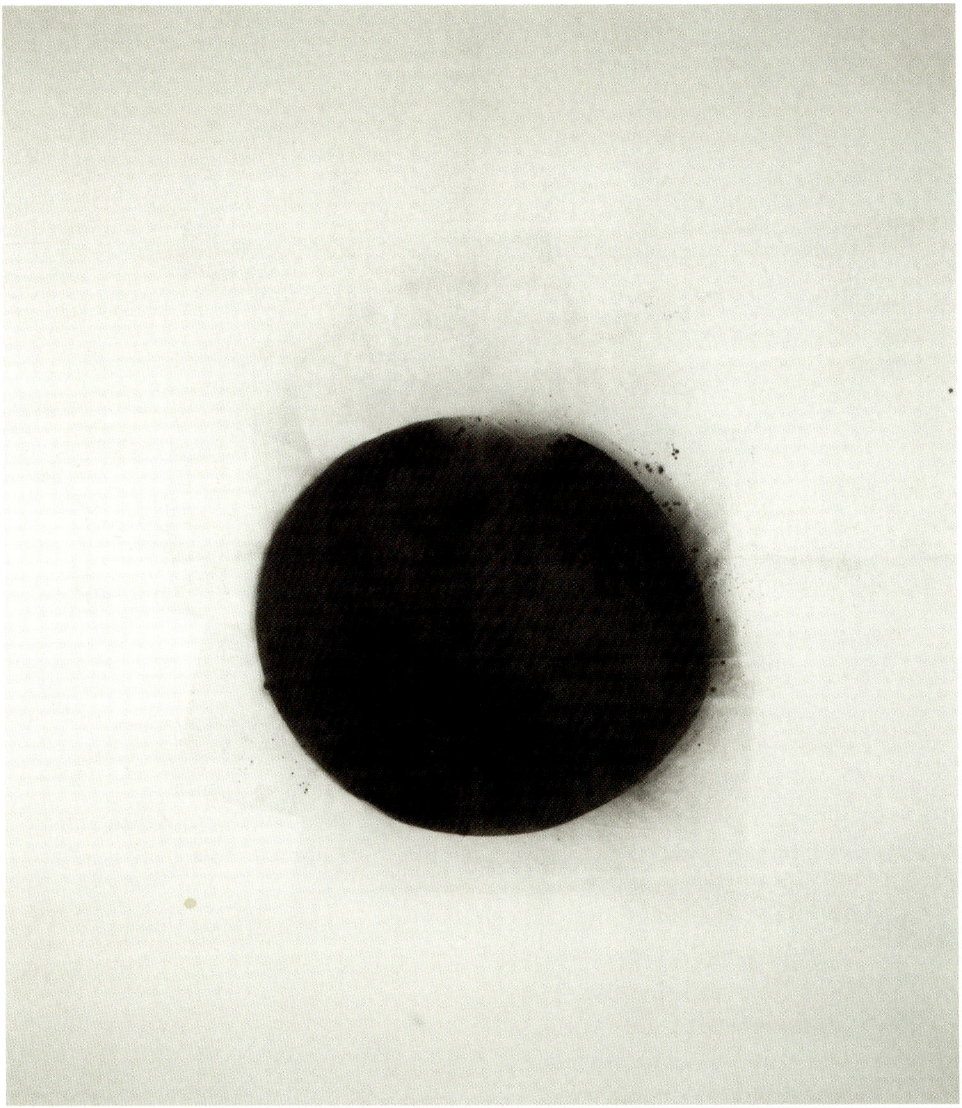

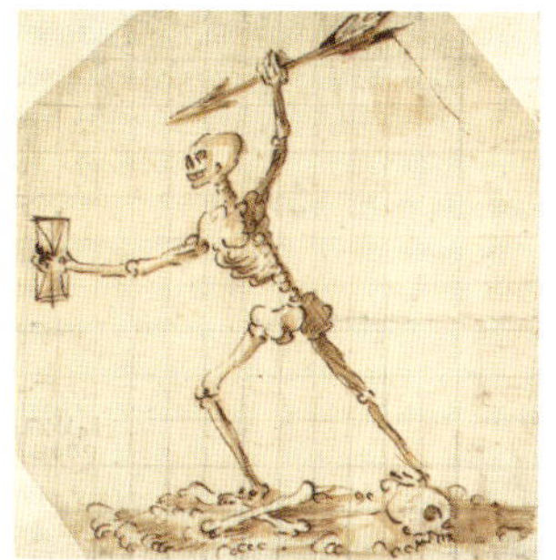

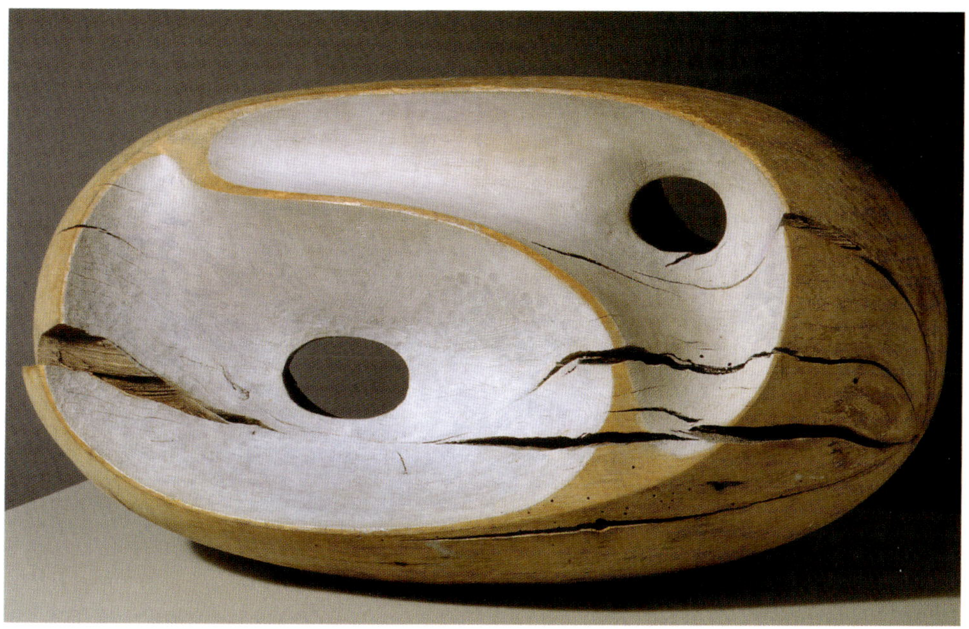

human activity would lead to ecological collapse, after which the biosphere would endure a period of shock, from which it would then slowly recover. In another, irreversible heating would lead to the evaporation of the oceans, and the end of life on earth.

The Earth's moon is unusually large relative to the size of the planet, and the tidal oscillations it causes lead to extensive intertidal zones with conditions that favour the emergence of life. The Moon is moving away from the Earth at 3.8 cm per year, and so has not always appeared to be the same size as the Sun. When it was closer, tidal movements would have been more extreme, and the conditions for life's emergence perhaps even more favourable.

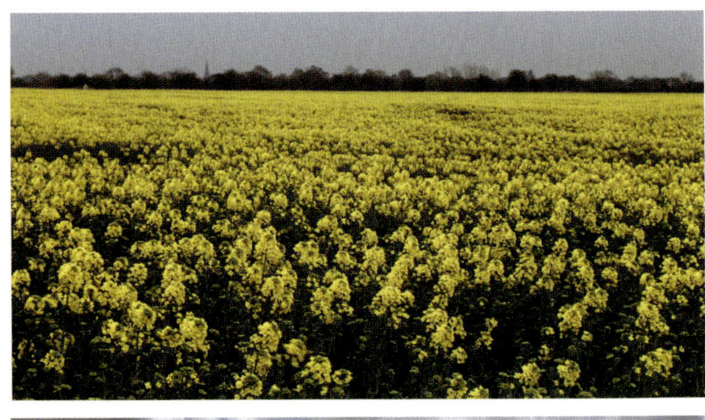
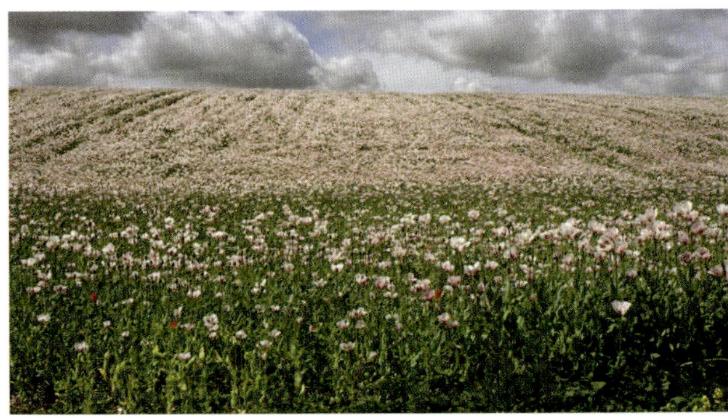
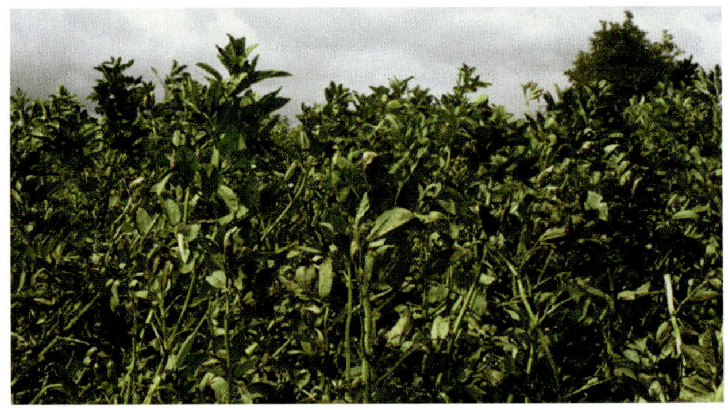
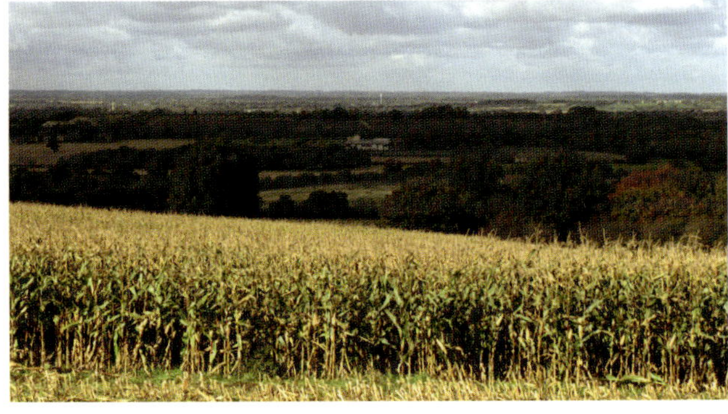

Robinson in Ruins: fields of oilseed rape, opium, field beans and maize

Agriculture

'Oilseed rape', he wrote, 'is a plant of the genus *brassica*. The name "rape" derives from the Latin for turnip, and was first recorded in English at the end of the fourteenth century, when the plant was a source of lamp oil. Rape seed oil was produced in the nineteenth century as a lubricant for steam engines.In 2007, the UK's production first exceeded 2 million tonnes, eleven per cent more than consumption for domestic uses which as well as cooking oil, include margarine, cattle feed, candles, soaps, plastics, polymers and lubricants. The main export trade is to Germany, for biodiesel.' At the time, rapeseed oil was the preferred oil stock for biodiesel production in most of Europe.

… in South Oxfordshire … several large farms had contracts to grow opium.

Though cultivated in Britain for over 3,000 years, field beans were grown in the UK mainly for animal feed. Field beans for human consumption were exported, mostly to Egypt, to be used in a variety of dishes, especially during Ramadan.

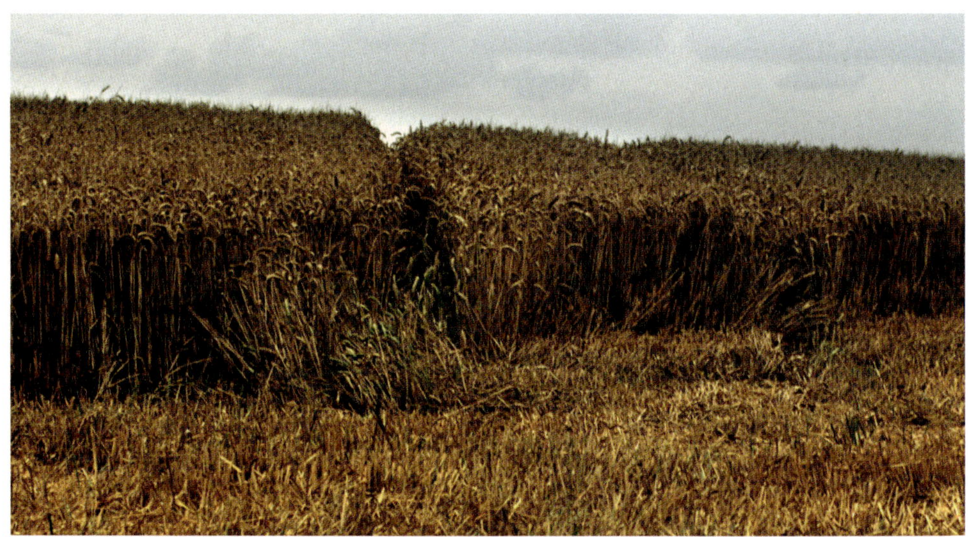

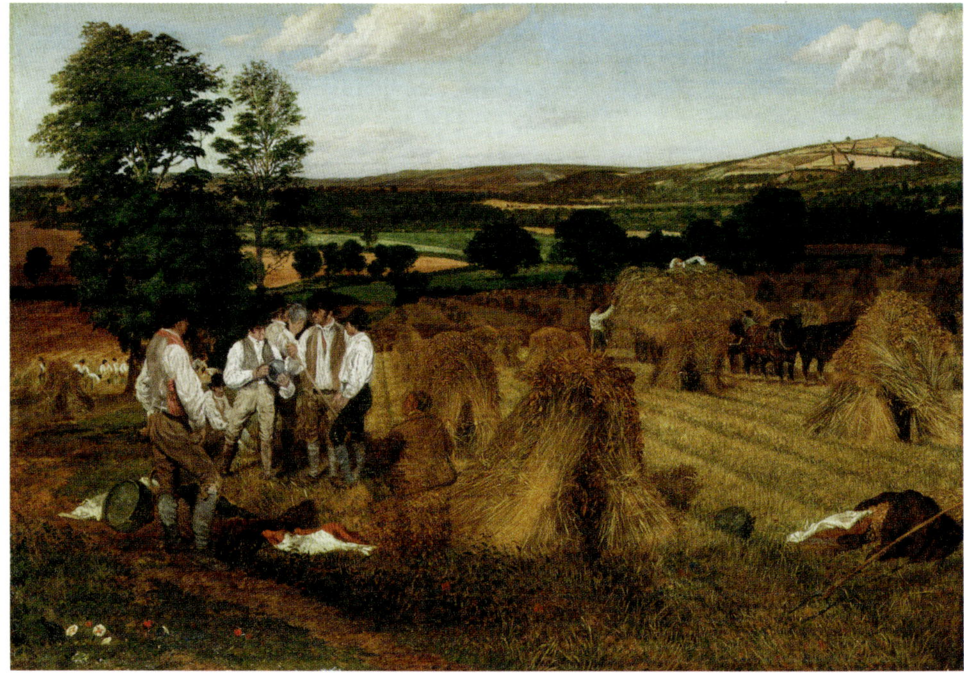

Robinson in Ruins

George Robert Lewis
*Hereford, Dynedor and the Malvern
Hills, from the Haywood Lodge,
Harvest Scene, Afternoon* 1815

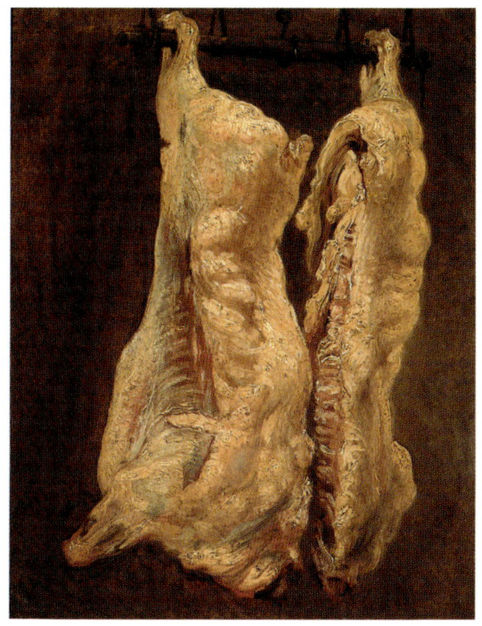

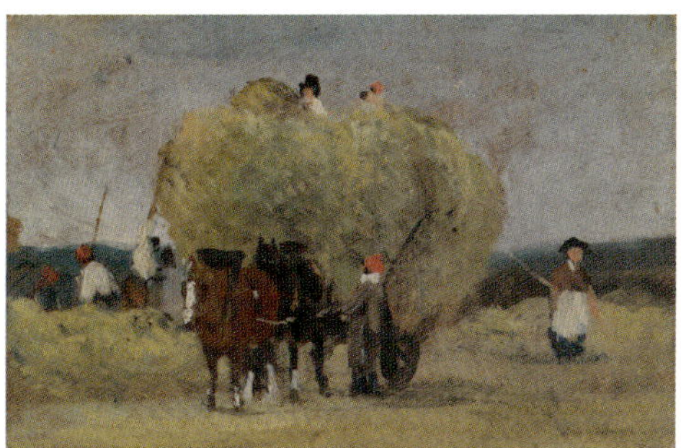

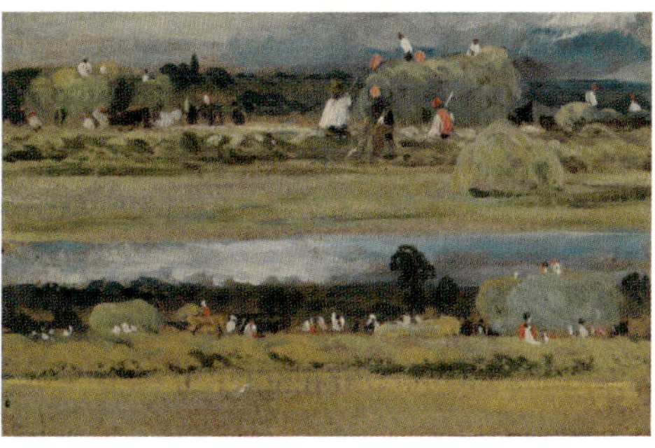

Wheat has been domesticated for at least ten
thousand years. It is the UK's predominant
crop, one of the world's three major staples.
In an average year, the UK grew about 15 million
tonnes of wheat, of which about twenty-five
per cent was exported. About forty per cent of
the crop was used as animal feed, much of it
for cattle. Only the best wheat could be sold,
at a higher price, for milling. Milling wheat
was typically about a third of the total harvest.

[On 16 October] a field of maize was harvested
for sileage.

Of the arable crops he'd encountered, apart from
opium, it appeared that none would be destined
primarily for human consumption.

Launton meteorite
(stone, ordinary chondrite)
Fell on 15 February 1830

Robinson in Ruins: a Millennium
Milepost of the type 'The
Cockerell', designed by Iain
McColl, seen in the film near
Launton

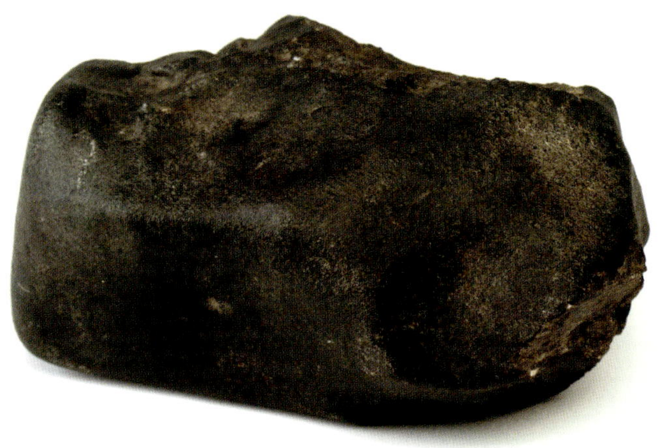

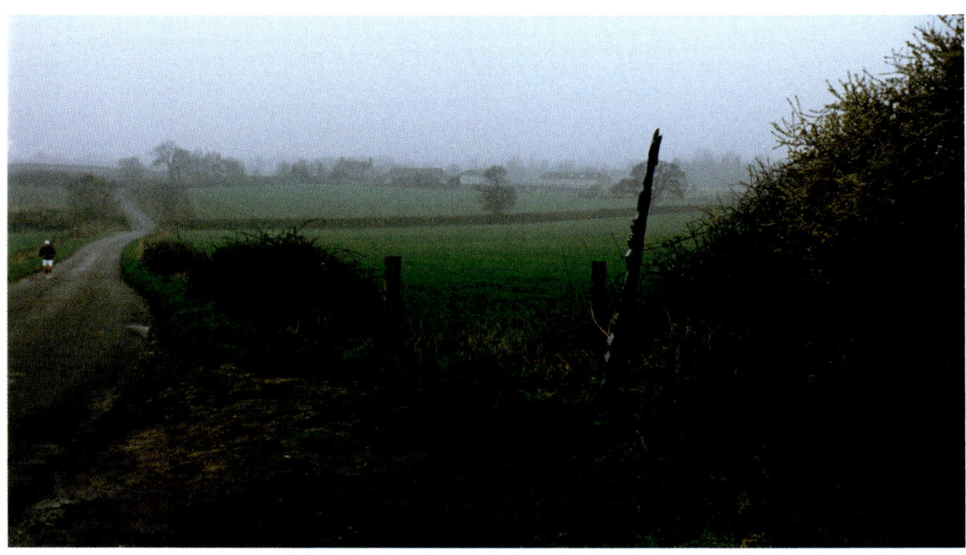

1830

On 20 April, he [had] walked to Launton, near
Bicester, in search of the site where a meteorite
fell on 15 February 1830. 1830 was a year of
revolutions, in France and Belgium, and in
England, where the Captain Swing riots began
at the end of August and continued through
the autumn. On 15 September, the Liverpool to
Manchester railway was inaugurated.

The monument was half way up Poundon Hill,
the site of a former Diplomatic Wireless Service
transmitter used by the Special Operations
Executive during World War II. But it was not
meant to commemorate the meteorite. It was
a 'Millennium Milepost' on a cycle route to
Cambridge, one of 1000 funded by the Royal
Bank of Scotland. RBS was the world's largest
bank. In the previous day's paper, he had read
about its weak capital position. It was then the
most vulnerable major bank in Europe.

A few months later, he was following a branch
of the GPSS pipeline, which ran parallel to the
former London to Aberystwyth coach road.

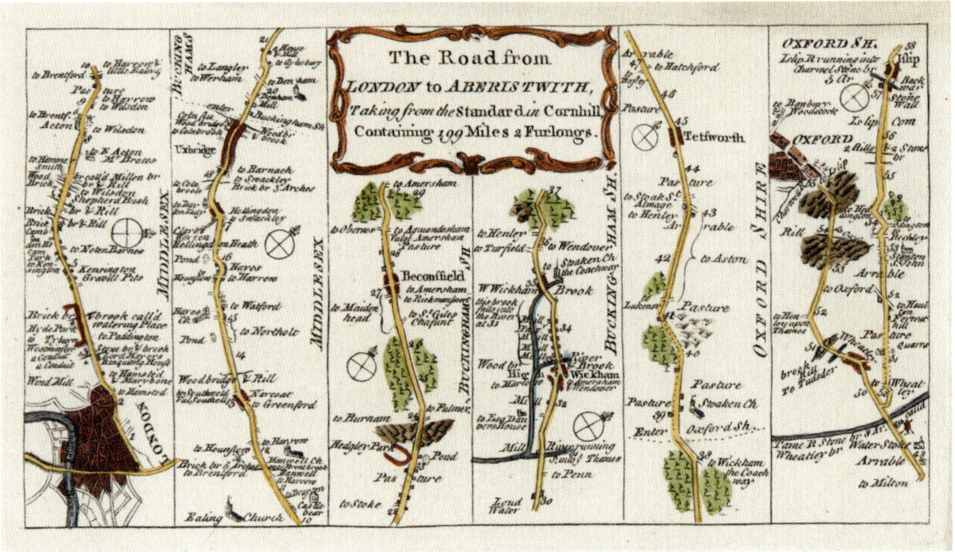

He was interested in the coach road. He sensed that it might lead him to an important destination, and decided to spend the rest of July in its vicinity.

There was a view, to the north-west, of another quarry, and a few miles further on, a distant chimney, which suggested the likelihood of romantic ruins.

At the next village, Islip, there was a fuel depot alongside the station. The US Air Force had left Upper Heyford in 1994, and the depot didn't seem to be in use, though it was maintained, perhaps in case of some anticipated emergency. The sign on the gate said 'Amalgamated Construction'. Amco was a UK-based group, which provided 'design, project-management and construction services' to the 'rail, energy, engineering and materials-handling markets'. By the end of the month, the price of oil had dropped below $125 a barrel.

Further on, the road passed near to Otmoor, the landscape of *Through the Looking Glass*.

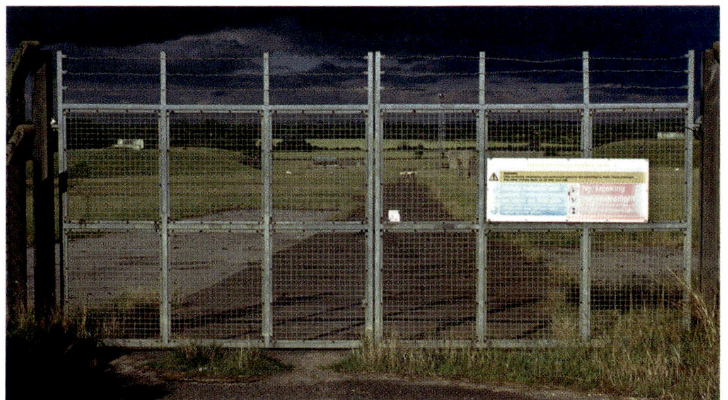

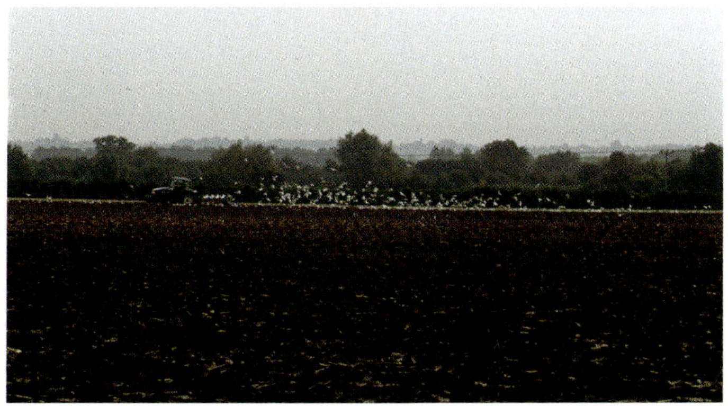

Otmoor was a wetland common, where the inhabitants of the 'seven towns' were accustomed to graze cattle, sheep and geese. When landlords had secured legislation for the moor's enclosure, the river Ray was rerouted, and began to flood neighbouring farms. In June 1830, farmers affected broke the New Channel's embankment; twenty-nine were charged with felony, but were acquitted, after pleading they had acted 'to relieve themselves of the inconvenience of having their lands overflowed by what the Commissioners had done'. The acquittals encouraged a belief that the enclosure lacked a legal basis: on Monday, 6 September, about a thousand people walked the circumference of the moor, 'possessioning' it, in accordance with a local custom, and destroyed every fence and hedge that they encountered. Yeomanry arrived, and a Mr Henley read the Riot Act, but the crowd did not disperse. Of sixty-six arrested, forty-four were sent, with an armed escort of Yeomanry, to be detained in Oxford Gaol. In the city, at the annual St Giles' Fair, a huge crowd was sympathetic to the protest.

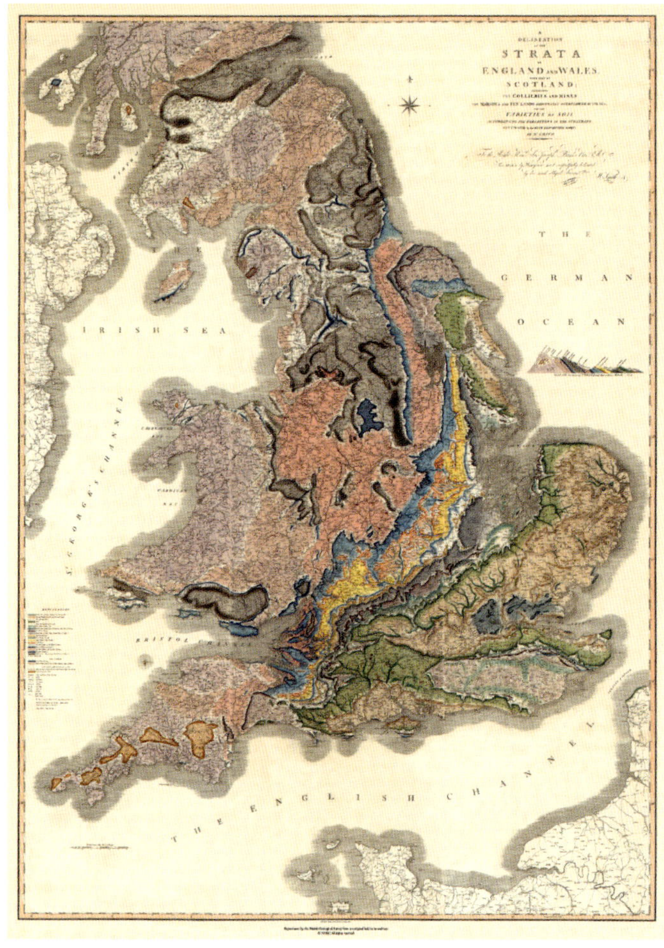

When the convoy arrived, the crowd attacked, and the prisoners were rescued. The resistance then acquired a pattern: on moonlit nights, large crowds would go out; with blackened faces, some of the men disguised as women, armed with pitchforks, bill-hooks and guns, they would pull down the enclosures that had been put up during the day. Troops failed to prevent the action from continuing. Between 1832 and 1835, a force of Metropolitan constables policed the moor, at a cost of thirteen per cent of the county's expenditure; there was anger that the public should protect a private property speculation. In time, the alliance of the property-owning farmers with their poorer neighbours weakened, and the fence-breaking subsided. The enclosure itself was largely unsuccessful.[25]

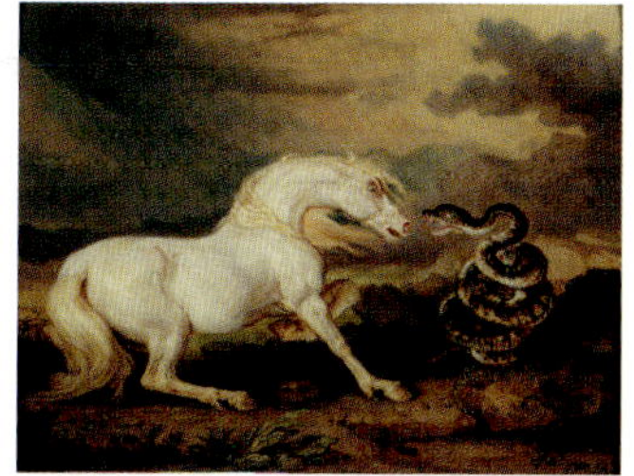

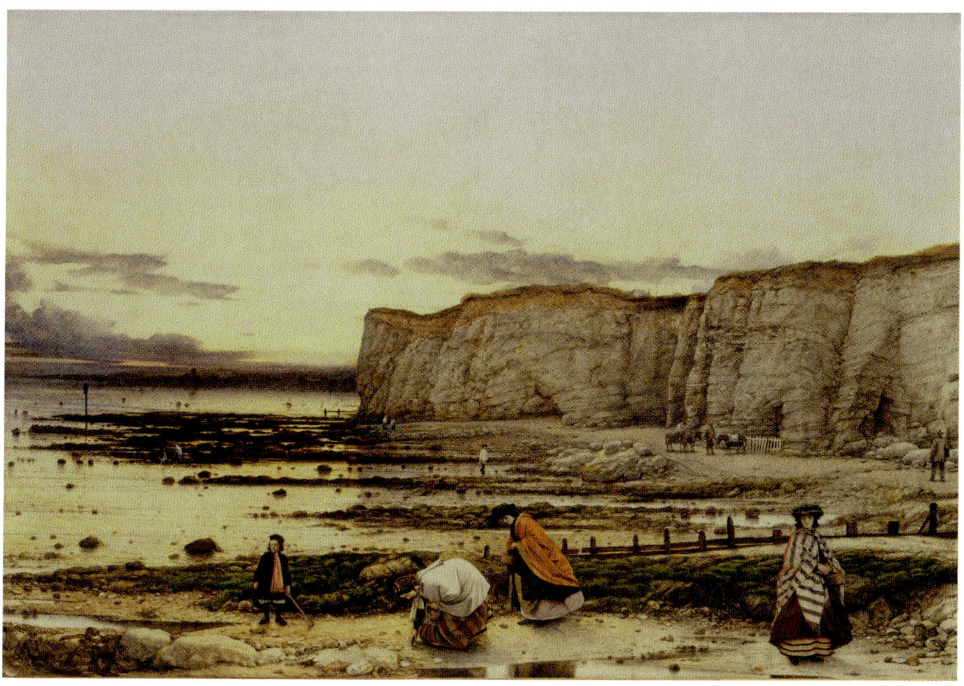

The first volume of Charles Lyell's *The Principles of Geology: Being an Attempt to Explain the Former Changes of the Earth's Surface, by Reference to Causes now in Operation* was published in 1830. Lyell's book described the long-term, slow-moving forces that had shaped the earth, establishing that the biblical timescale of creation was no longer credible.

25. See Bernard Reaney, *The Class Struggle in 19th-century Oxfordshire: The Social and Communal Background to the Otmoor Disturbances of 1830 to 1835*, Oxford 1970; David Eastwood, 'Communities, Protest and Police in early Nineteenth-Century Oxfordshire: The Enclosure of Otmoor Reconsidered', *Agricultural History Review*, vol.44, no.1, 1996, pp.35–46.

Robinson in Ruins: cement works
and limestone quarry, Shipton-
on-Cherwell

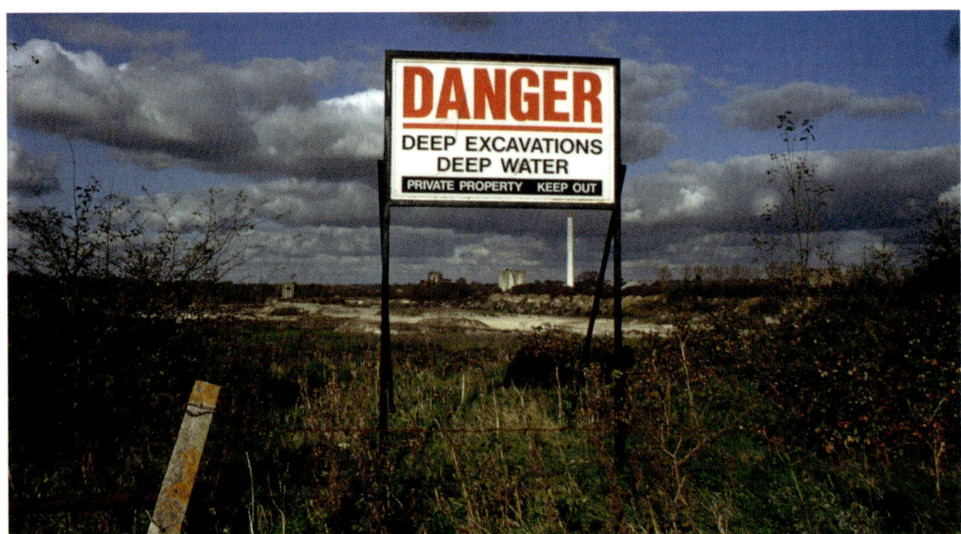

DANGER
DEEP EXCAVATIONS
DEEP WATER
PRIVATE PROPERTY   KEEP OUT

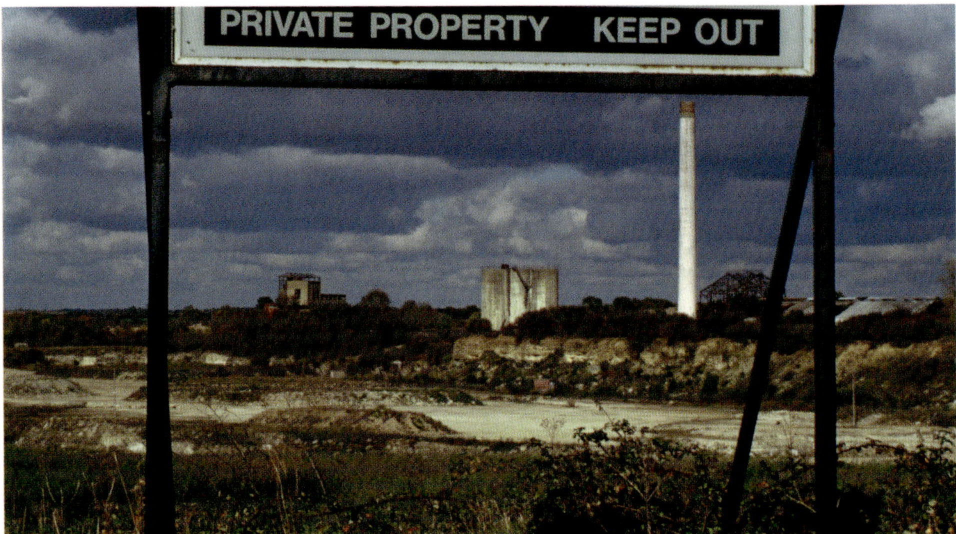

PRIVATE PROPERTY   KEEP OUT

Destination

In recent decades, in the UK and other similar economies, median incomes have risen very little, if at all, while inequality has increased sharply. The richest groups in these societies have acted very successfully to transfer wealth to themselves from the poor and the middle class. The rise of the super-rich during the last few decades was described as long ago as 1997 as 'a seminal development in modern Britain, as critical as the rise of the gentry before the English Civil War'[26] – the unsettled period of the 'Jacobean Melancholy'. Many of these landowners became wealthy through enclosure, depriving their poorer neighbours of what had been, until then, customary rights to land. The recent period has involved a comparable dispossession. This curious change, aided by governments and accompanied by the relentless ideological promotion of selected individual freedoms at the expense of previously hard-won collective assets and social fabric, has involved a revival of the fallacy that markets are spontaneously-occurring, 'natural' phenomena.

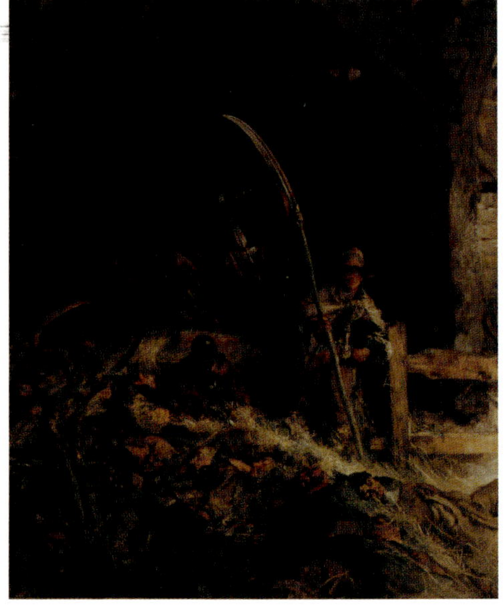

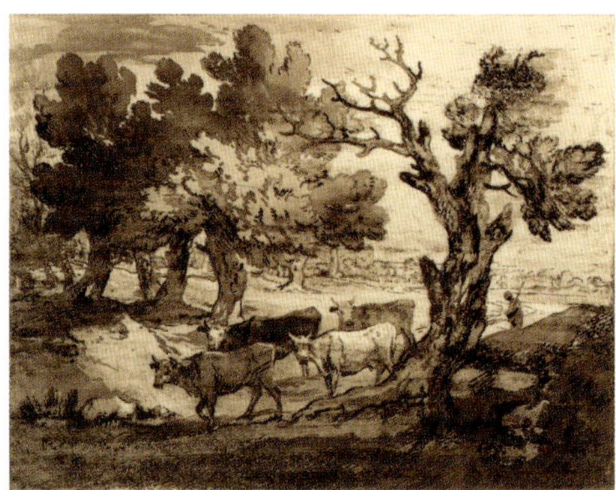

In the autumn of 2008, however, after the collapse of Lehman Brothers and the government interventions that followed, 'it seemed possible, for a moment, to imagine this was no ordinary crisis, and that some larger, historic shift might be occurring'.

Robinson had followed the London to Aberystwyth road to Enslow, where it crosses the river Cherwell.

On 8 October, he left the road and set out in the direction of the ruined factory, but came instead to Hampton Gay, which he recognised as a *deserted village*.

A notice stated that 'late in the reign of Elizabeth I, enclosure of the land by "new gentry" proved disastrous for the inhabitants, who banded together in 1596' in an abortive rising.[27] There had been three poor harvests, and by autumn the price of grain had doubled since the beginning of the year.

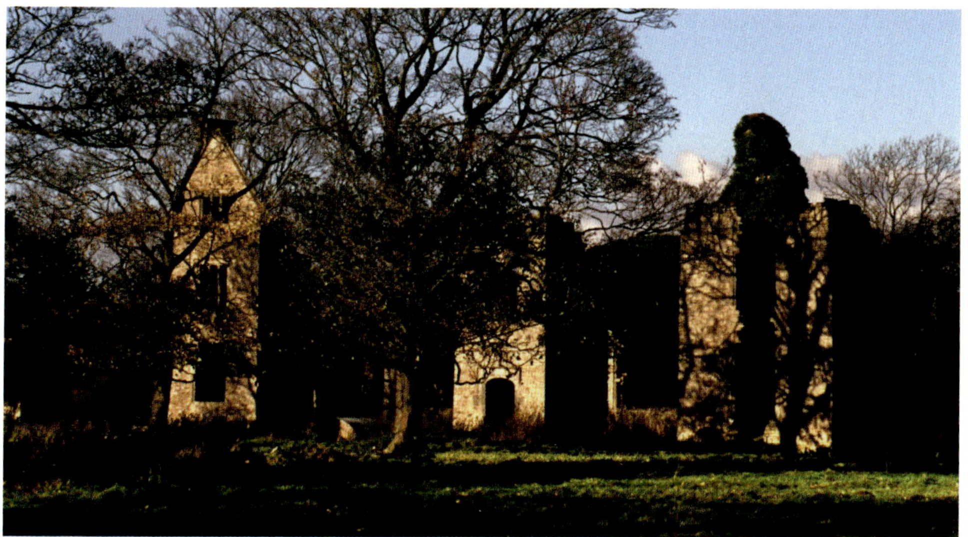

The village's landlord was Vincent Barry.
His grandfather John had bought the manor for
£1,100, in 1544. A former glover, he had become
rich grazing sheep on land acquired after the
dissolution of the monasteries. By 1596, the Barrys
had enclosed much of the manor, and built the
manor house. It was gutted by a fire in 1887.

Bartholomew Steer was a twenty-eight-year-old
carpenter who had worked for Barry, and lived
in the village. With a few companions, he had
travelled to nearby villages and towns, preaching

'the politics of Cockayne': '"Work? Care not for
worke, for we shall have a meryer world shortly"
... "There would be a rising of the people to
pulle downe the enclosures" ... they "needed
not to worke, nor take anie care for Corne this
deere yeare", for they would "pull the corne out
of the Riche men's barnes".' They planned an
armed progress through the county, knocking
down gentlemen. At Vincent Barry's, they would
'"spoill him and Cutt off his heade"'.[28]

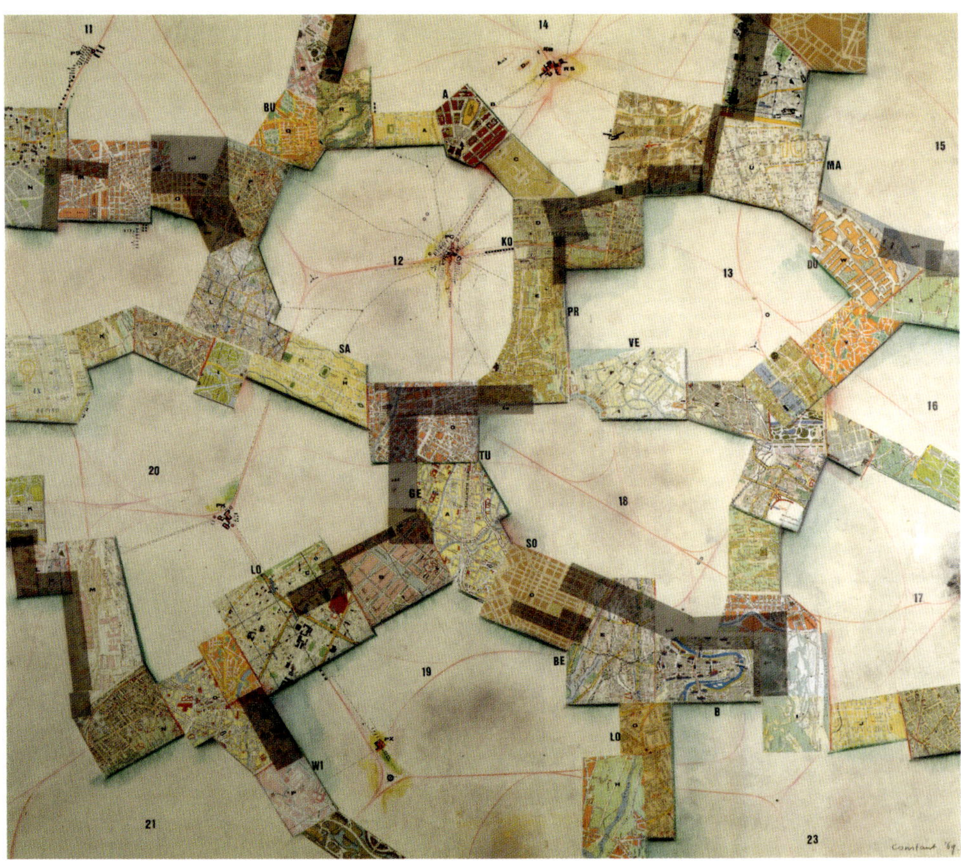

Steer called for the rising to assemble at Enslow Hill at 9 o'clock on the evening of Sunday 21 November, but only three men joined him. After these four and several others had been arrested and examined under torture, two survivors were hanged, drawn and quartered on the hill. In 1597, however, the Privy Council began a series of prosecutions of the most notorious enclosers and in Parliament, Francis Bacon introduced two bills: *An Act against the Decaying of Towns and Houses of Husbandry* and *An Act for the Maintenance of Husbandry and Tillage*, that became law in 1598.

On the opposite bank of the river Cherwell, beside the Great Western Railway and the Oxford Canal, is the quarry of the former Shipton-on-Cherwell cement works.

On 17 October, when Robinson revisited the ruined cement works, he encountered a moment of experiential transformation.

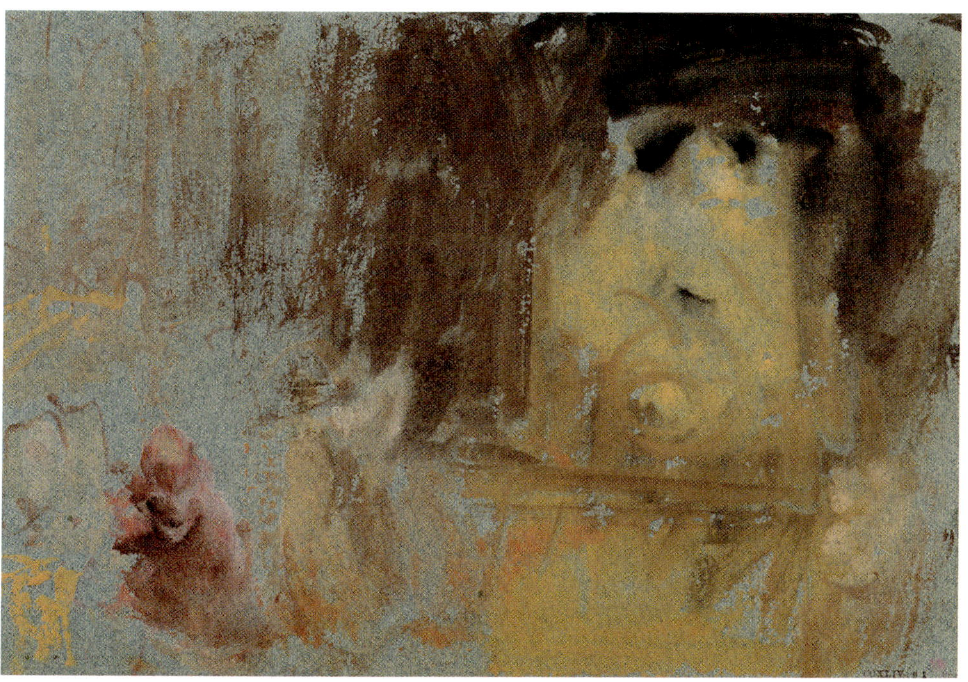

A few days later, he made contact with our research team. He proposed that we establish an experimental settlement: in spaces of extraordinary biomorphic architecture, we would devise ways to reform land ownership and democratic government; we would pioneer the renewal of industry and agriculture, after the decline of the global dollar, and the disappearance of cheap oil.

26. Andrew Adonis and Stephen Pollard, *A Class Act: The Myth of Britain's Classless Society*, London 1997, p.67.
27. See John Walter, 'A "Rising of the People"? The Oxfordshire Rising of 1596', *Past and Present*, no.107, May 1985, pp.90–143, reprinted in John Walter, *Crowds and Popular Politics in Early Modern England*, Manchester 2006, pp.73–123.
28. Ibid., pp. 90, 100.

First published 2012 by order of the Tate Trustees
by Tate Publishing, a division of Tate Enterprises Ltd,
Millbank, London SW1P 4RG

www.tate.org.uk/publishing

British Library Cataloguing in Publication Data
A catalogue record for this book is available from
the British Library

ISBN: 978 1 84976 072 0

Colour reproduction by DL Imaging Ltd, London
Printed in Italy by Graphicom

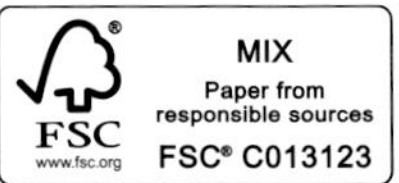

Acknowledgements

Patrick Keiller gratefully acknowledges support from
the Arts and Humanities Research Council, the Royal
College of Art, the Calouste Gulbenkian Foundation
and the British Film Institute in realising *Robinson in
Ruins*, and the assistance of Julie Norris throughout.

Photo credits

Reproduced by permission of the
British Geological Survey. © NERC 2008,
all rights reserved. IPR/145-67CT 56

© The British Library Board (Maps.28.c.47) 11

Collection of Gemeentemuseum Den Haag,
The Hague, The Netherlands 62

Courtesy Hammer/Exclusive Media 25

Patrick Keiller cover, 2, 4, 17, 18, 19, 20, 27, 28,
31 bottom, 33 top, 34 bottom, 38, 39, 40, 44, 48,
50 top, 52 bottom, 55, 58, 61

John Mckenzie 7

© Manchester City Galleries 14

The National Archives, Kew 22

The Natural History Museum, London
31 top, 52

Julie Norris 13

Parliamentary Archives, London HL/PO/
PU/1/1795/35G3n239 30

Rolls Royce photo lab 21

Tate Photography 8, 9, 10, 15, 24, 32 top,
33 bottom, 34 top, 35, 36, 41, 46, 47, 50 bottom,
51 top, 57, 60, 63

Tate Photography/Mark Heathcote 51 bottom

Tate Photography/Rod Tidnam 26, 42, 43, 54

Copyright

All images © Patrick Keiller except
where stated otherwise

© The estate of Sir Muirhead Bone.
All rights reserved, DACS 2012 9

© SK Stiftung Kultur, Bonn.
All rights reserved, DACS 2012 7

© Bowness, Hepworth Estate 46 top,
47 bottom

© 1957 Clarion Films Ltd. Copyright renewed
1985 by Hammer Film Productions Ltd 25

Crown Copyright 22

© DACS, 2012 10, 62

© The estate of Nigel Henderson 8

© Peter Kennard 36

© Bryan Kneale 24

© The estate of John Latham (noit prof.
of flattime), courtesy Lisson Gallery, London
46 bottom

© Julie Norris 13

Credits for Tate works

7 ARTIST ROOMS Tate and National Galleries
of Scotland. Lent by Anthony d'Offay 2010

8 Presented by Colin St John Wilson 1975

9 Presented by Sir Michael Sadler through
the Art Fund 1931

10 Presented by Mr and Mr Robert Lewin
through the Friends of the Tate Gallery 1987

15 Accepted by the nation as part of the
Turner Bequest 1856

24 Purchased 1967

32 top Accepted by the nation as part of
the Turner Bequest 1856

33 bottom Transferred from the British
Museum 1988

34 top Presented by Paul Mellon through
the British Sporting Art Trust 1979

35 top Presented by A. Acland Allen through
the Art Fund 1925

35 bottom Accepted by the nation as part
of the Turner Bequest 1856

36 Purchased from the artist 2007

41 Presented by the War Artists Advisory
Committee 1946

46 top Presented by Curwen Studio through
the Institute of Contemporary Prints 1975

46 bottom Presented by Nicholas Logsdail
and Lisson Gallery, London 2005

47 top Purchased as part of the Oppé
Collection with assistance from the
National Lottery

47 bottom Presented by Ben Nicholson OM
1975

50 bottom Presented by the Rev. Stopford
Brooke 1904

51 top Purchased 1942

51 bottom Presented by Mrs M. Bernard
1973

57 top Purchased 1982

57 bottom Purchased 1894

60 top Presented by the Trustees of
the Chantrey Bequest 1905

60 bottom Purchased 1971

63 Accepted by the nation as part of
the Turner Bequest 1856